March 15, 2, 000
Vance

Traveling To Twelve Historic Monuments

Following A Route
Of History

Vance W. Snyder

Fairway Press, Lima, Ohio

TRAVELING TO TWELVE HISTORIC MONUMENTS

FIRST EDITION
Copyright © 1999
Vance W. Snyder

ISBN 0-7880-1447-1   PRINTED IN U.S.A.

DEDICATION

*To the memory of
my wife of many years,
Gertrude B. Snyder
1911-1996*

Table Of Contents

Preface

The twelve historic monuments indicated by the title of this book are the Madonna of the Trail Monuments. These were situated on The National Old Trails Road.

The road designated as The National Old Trails Road has not existed under this name for several decades. This name was made obsolete by the system of numbering highways that has been in effect for many years.

It was the National Society of the Daughters of the American Revolution that placed these twelve monuments, during the 1920's, in the states of Maryland, Pennsylvania, West Virginia, Ohio, Indiana, Illinois, Missouri, Kansas, Colorado, New Mexico, Arizona, and California.

Beginning on 4 July, 1928, and ending on 19 April, 1929, the twelve monuments were dedicated. The one farthest east is at Bethesda, Maryland, and the monument farthest west is at Upland, California.

I first became interested in these monuments a number of years ago. On a vacation trip, my wife, Gertrude, and I saw our first Madonna Monument in one of the midwestern states. At a later time, we saw the one in eastern Arizona, the monument nearest our home in Tucson, Arizona.

At the library, I was able to get some information about The National Old Trails Road, and we began to plan a trip that would follow this route, and that would take us to the twelve monuments.

We decided that on our next trip to the eastern states, we would make a project of visiting all of the monuments when we made our return to the West. Our plan was to make it a coast-to-coast trip by starting at a point on the Atlantic coast. We would go to Bethesda, Maryland, and visit the first monument. After traveling across the country to California, we would visit the twelfth monument at Upland, then continue to a point on the Pacific coast.

Late in the spring, we drove to Ohio and visited our daughter in Columbus. We have relatives in northern Ohio, and in Erie, Pennsylvania; after several days in Columbus, we went north in Ohio. We stayed there about a week, then drove northeast to Erie.

Traveling to the southeast across Pennsylvania from Erie, we reached the state of Delaware, near the city of Wilmington. Here we turned to the south, drove through Dover, the state capital, then continued to the starting point of our trip.

On a day in early July, we left the coast of Delaware and started on our long trip to the West. This cross-country travel took us into several cities, towns, and villages. These can be found on highway maps.

It will be noted that population figures are shown for many of the cities on our route of travel. The reason that this has been done is to show the development and growth of these cities since the earliest time of settlement. In the same time period, towns and villages in the region developed more slowly, or, in some instances, may have disappeared.

Chapter 1

Delaware

Rehoboth Beach, the city we selected as the starting point of our coast-to-coast trip, lies directly on the Atlantic Ocean.

Once in November, while we were living in Ohio, we traveled to the Delaware coast and stayed at Rehoboth Beach for two nights, but did not visit Lewes, several miles to the northwest.

On this summer day of our present trip, when we came south through Delaware, we drove to Lewes in mid-morning so we could see this historic town. Our first stop was at the Visitors Bureau, and the booklet distributed there states that Lewes is "The First Town in the First State."

The Constitutional Convention, called to draw up a Constitution for the United States after the War for Independence, met in Philadelphia in May, 1787. Its work was finished in September of that year. Ratification of the Constitution depended on the approval of at least nine states.

Delegates from Delaware met at Dover and ratified the Constitution on Friday, December 7, 1787, five days before the Pennsylvania convention cast its vote for ratification. Thus, Delaware became the first state to enter the Union. Wherever Delaware automobiles are driven, their license plates proclaim that Delaware is the First State.

In December, 1630, a vessel sailed from a port in Holland. It carried a cargo of provisions, merchandise, equipment, and livestock, and aboard were 28 colonists in addition to the crew. In the early spring of 1631, the vessel landed near present-day Lewes and the colonists established a small settlement that they named Zwaanendael. This settlement near the mouth of Delaware Bay was the first European colony in what is now the state of Delaware.

Because of an unfortunate misunderstanding with local Indians, the settlement was destroyed and the colonists were massacred several months after the colony was started. A few years later, a lasting European colony in Delaware was set up by Swedish settlers at a point farther north.

By the 1670s, a port was operating at the present site of Lewes and many colonists from England had settled in the area. The town was named after Lewes, Sussex, England.

The Zwaanendael Museum in Lewes was dedicated in 1931, the 300th anniversary of the founding of this first European settlement in Delaware. The building is very similar to the Town Hall in Hoorn, Holland. The architect studied the building at Hoorn before drawing up the plans. There are permanent displays, as well as changing exhibits, that depict the history of Lewes and the surrounding area.

During the War of 1812, a British squadron shelled the town of Lewes on April 6 and 7, 1813. Unable to bring their ships within cannon range because of shallow water offshore, little damage was done. One small cannonball struck the foundation of the building that is known as the Cannonball House. It is now the Cannonball House Marine Museum with many nautical exhibits.

Saint Peter's Episcopal Church has a history dating back to the early 1700s when the first church was built. A second building was erected soon after 1800 and the present building was dedicated in 1858.

In the churchyard, the oldest stone marks the grave of a woman born in 1631 and whose death occurred in 1707. Four men who served as governors of Delaware are buried here, along with judges and members of the legislature. Also in the churchyard is the grave of an English sea captain whose ship went down off Lewes in 1798.

After our visit to Lewes and enjoying lunch there, we went to Rehoboth Beach early in the afternoon. As mentioned before, our previous visit here was in late autumn. Our main reason for traveling to the coast at that time was to see the birds that wintered in this area. We spent the daytime hours observing the birds on a long stretch of beach and on the nearby waters.

As we drove down a street that led toward the ocean, in the afternoon of this July day, parking places were scarce, but we were fortunate in finding an open parking meter that was within a short walk of the beach. Hundreds of people were sunbathing and many were shielded from the sun by their colorful beach umbrellas. Others were wading in the surf, and some were swimming or riding the incoming waves. From our vantage point, I took photographs of the crowded beach with the vast Atlantic Ocean on the horizon. We remembered the nearly deserted beach of those days in late autumn on our previous visit here, and there was no resemblance to the present scene. On the way back to our car, we visited two or three of the shops along the busy street and made some small purchases.

The municipality was named Rehoboth by the legislature in 1893, and it was officially named "The City of Rehoboth Beach" in April, 1937.

The origin of the name "Rehoboth" is found in the Bible, (Genesis: chapter 26, verse 22), and nearby Rehoboth Bay was named in the seventeenth century.

This popular seaside resort on the Delaware Coast is almost directly east of Washington, D.C. The Chesapeake Bay Bridge makes it easier to go there from this capital city of the United States, as well as from Baltimore and other points to the west of Chesapeake Bay.

After staying part of the afternoon, we left Rehoboth Beach, and a few miles out of the city brought us to the highway that we took to Georgetown and points west. Most of the First State is situated in the Atlantic Coastal Plain, and, of the fifty states, only Rhode Island is smaller in area.

There are three counties in Delaware, and of these, New Castle County occupies the northern part of the state. It has the smallest land area and the largest population of the three counties. Wilmington, the county seat, is the largest city in Delaware. The state's highest point, 442 feet above sea level, is a few miles north of Wilmington, in the Piedmont foothills, and very close to the Delaware-Pennsylvania boundary.

Kent County, with a land area somewhat larger than its neighbor to the north, is in the center of the state. Dover is the county seat, as well as the capital of Delaware. The town was laid out in the early 1700s, and later in the century was made the capital city.

Sussex County is in the southern portion of Delaware, and its land area is almost half the total area of the state. Georgetown, the county seat, is situated in farming country, about sixteen miles from the Atlantic Ocean. We noted the highway sign at the entrance to the town that stated in large letters, "HISTORIC GEORGETOWN — HURRY BACK!" Roads to the neighboring countryside radiate from the town's traffic circle.

The town was established soon after 1790, when it was decided that the county seat should be placed in the center of the county. After the land was purchased and the courthouse was built, the village slowly began to grow. George Mitchell was one of the commissioners who were in charge of founding the new county seat, and Georgetown was named in his honor.

Beyond Georgetown, our route was through level farmland in which corn seemed to be the principal crop. We soon came to Bridgeville, a town that had its beginning in 1730 when a bridge was built over a branch of the Nanticoke River. Several miles northwest of Bridgeville, our trip through Delaware came to an end, as we crossed the state boundary.

Chapter 2

Maryland

The first settlers in the state of Maryland left England on November 22, 1633. The two small ships that were carrying them crossed the Atlantic Ocean, stopped briefly in the West Indies, then sailed north along the Atlantic Coast. On March 25, 1634, the colonists went ashore on an island near the mouth of the Potomac River.

From this initial population of about 150, the number of people in Maryland increased to approximately 43,000 in 1710. A large percentage of this population inhabited the area that borders Chesapeake Bay.

As we entered Caroline County, Maryland, the sign at the state boundary line greeted us with polite words of caution, "Maryland Welcomes You. Please Drive Gently." About a dozen miles farther on we crossed the Choptank River at Denton, the county seat. This was named Eden Town, for Sir Robert Eden, colonial governor of Maryland under the British. The name was soon shortened to Edenton, then evolved to its present form when the first letter of the name was omitted.

A brief stop was made at the town of Queen Anne on our way to Wye Mills.

Wye Oak State Park is adjacent to Wye Mills and is the site of the Wye Oak. A plaque mounted on a post near the tree says, "The largest white oak in the United States. Estimated to be 400 years old (1940). Deeded to the State of Maryland, Sept. 20, 1939, and made a state park."

This venerable giant was nearly one hundred years old when the first settlers came to Maryland. The state tree is the white oak; it is appropriate that this state park has been set aside for the people of Maryland and for visitors to the state.

From Wye Mills we returned to the highway that took us to Kent Island and to the bridge that extends across Chesapeake Bay from the island to Sandy Point on the western shore. The construction of the William Preston Lane, Jr. Memorial Bridge was finished in 1952. In 1973, a bridge parallel to the original structure was completed.

At a junction point about ten miles from the western end of the Bay bridge, a main highway goes in a northwesterly direction to Baltimore. Annapolis, the state capital of Maryland, as well as the county seat of Anne Arundel County, is a few miles southwest of this highway junction. The city is situated on the Severn River near its entrance into Chesapeake Bay. Early in its history, this town that later became the capital city was called, variously, Providence, Severn, and Anne Arundel. The latter name was from the name of the county that was set up in 1650. The town received its present name, Annapolis, in 1695.

In May, 1775, the Continental Congress met in Philadelphia to determine what action the colonies should take toward Great Britain. Early in June, the Congress authorized the formation of the Continental Army. On June 15, 1775, George Washington was appointed commander in chief, a position he held throughout the American Revolution. Most hostilities in this long war ceased on October 19, 1781, when the British commander, Lord Cornwallis, surrendered at Yorktown, Virginia.

Early in 1783, a group of Annapolis citizens joined with the Maryland Assembly in an attempt to have the Congress name Annapolis as the capital of the new confederation of states. When the Maryland resolutions were presented to Congress, it was decided to accept the offer, at least for the time being. As a result of this action, the Continental Congress held its sessions in Annapolis from November 26, 1783, to June 3, 1784. The Maryland State House has the distinction of being the only State House in the country that served as the Capital of the Unites States. During this period some memorable events took place here.

On December 23, 1783, General George Washington resigned his commission as commander in chief of the Continental Army. It was an impressive occasion at the Maryland State House, as General Washington made a brief speech and then turned in his commission. After eight years he was a private citizen again and returned to his home at Mount Vernon in Virginia.

14

Just over three weeks after this event, on January 14, 1784, the Revolutionary War was officially ended when the Treaty of Paris was ratified in this State House.

Besides being the state capital, Annapolis is the home of the United States Naval Academy with its several thousand naval personnel. A guided tour of the Academy, with an opportunity to visit the chapel, makes it possible for the visitor to see the John Paul Jones' crypt.

From its beginning late in the 17th century, Annapolis developed into a city with a population of 33,195 in 1990.

Maryland was one of the thirteen colonies that fought Great Britain in the War for Independence and as one of the thirteen original states entered the Union on April 28, 1788.

We followed the main highway north toward Baltimore from the junction mentioned previously and went through Arnold, Severna Park, Pasadena, Glen Burnie, and other communities. Our destination was Fort McHenry National Monument and Historic Shrine. On previous trips to eastern Maryland we had not visited this National Monument.

After we arrived here we saw the interesting film and toured the fort. Fort McHenry was named for James McHenry, an American officer during the Revolutionary War. Later, he was Secretary of War during part of President Washington's second term of office and in the Administration of President John Adams.

The War of 1812 was fought on several fronts, with land battles or naval engagements as far north as Canada and as far south as Florida and Louisiana. In late August, 1814, British troops occupied Washington, D.C., and burned much of the national capital, including several important government buildings. About three weeks after this military action, British warships sailed up Chesapeake Bay and attacked Fort McHenry, which protected Baltimore. This fort was constructed over a period of several years, from 1794 to about 1803.

The bombardment started early in the morning of September 13, 1814, and continued for more than 24 hours. Soon after daybreak on September 14, the shelling ceased and the fleet withdrew, leaving the fort and Baltimore in American hands.

15

Francis Scott Key, 35 years old, was a successful lawyer living in Washington at the time the British occupied the capital. Soon after this he was sent to negotiate the return of a doctor held by the British. Key was accompanied by a government official, and, after conferring with officers of the British fleet, the doctor was released. Because the attack on Fort McHenry was about to begin, the three Americans were held on a truce ship and remained there while the fort was bombarded. From this ship they were able to see the fort and they could see the shells from the time they were fired until they fell.

During the exciting hours of the attack, Francis Scott Key wrote parts of a poem and finished it a day or two later. It was published and soon was set to music and became "The Star-Spangled Banner." After more than a century, on March 3, 1931, this officially became the National Anthem of the United States by an Act of Congress.

After our visit to Fort McHenry we left Baltimore and traveled westward to Catonsville. In the beginning, this suburb of Baltimore was named Johnnycake, but nearly two centuries ago it was renamed for Richard Caton, owner of a large tract of land that included the townsite.

Ellicott City, county seat of Howard County, is located a few miles west of Catonsville on the Patapsco River. Andrew Ellicott was a Quaker who came from England to eastern Pennsylvania in 1730. His three sons settled at the present site of Ellicott City in 1774 and established a flour mill there. From the beginning, a town slowly developed over the next half-century, and growth was rapid after the railroad arrived in 1830.

Our route west from here was through West Friendship, Cooksville, Lisbon, Poplar Springs, and other communities. At New Market, a sign near the highway announces the year it was founded. In large letters and numbers the sign reads, "NEW MARKET — 1793." After a brief stop here we soon arrived at Frederick.

The region through which we had traveled after we left the Delaware Coast is mostly level. Frederick, with an elevation of approximately 300 feet above sea level, is in the Frederick Valley, drained by the Monocacy River.

At the Visitor Center, located near a main intersection in the center of the city, we were given directions to Mount Olivet Cemetery where we would be able to see the Francis Scott Key Monument. Mount Olivet is a large cemetery and this impressive memorial is located near the cemetery entrance.

The author of "The Star-Spangled Banner" was born August 1, 1779, near Keysville, Maryland. After graduating from Saint John's College in Annapolis in 1796 he studied law. His first law practice was opened in 1801 and he moved to the District of Columbia in 1805 to become a law partner with his uncle. Key was an active church member and he wrote a number of hymns. His death occurred in Baltimore on January 11, 1843, and he was buried there.

In 1898 the Monument was erected at the cemetery in Frederick. The remains of Francis Scott Key and his wife were moved from Baltimore and interred here.

The city of Frederick was established in 1745, three years prior to the formation of the county of the same name, and was incorporated in 1817. It is the county seat and is the marketing center for the large farming area that surrounds the city.

In the course of the Civil War, 1861-1865, Union infantry and cavalry units moved through Frederick on many occasions. Confederate troops entered the town for a period of a few days in each of the years 1862, 1863, and 1864.

On September 14, 1862 a battle was fought at South Mountain, northwest of Frederick. Here the Union army outnumbered the southern forces, and, in a daylong fight, the Southerners were forced to withdraw. During this Battle of South Mountain, Colonel Rutherford B. Hayes, future president of the United States (1877-1881), was wounded as he led a charge near the summit of the mountain. Taken first to a field hospital, then moved to a neighboring town, Hayes later returned to Ohio on leave until the wound healed.

At the time of the Battle of Gettysburg in early July, 1863, detachments of troops from the armies of the North and the South moved through Frederick. The routes followed by the main armies were at a distance from the town, so it was mostly undisturbed.

In early July, 1864, Frederick was directly involved in military action. On Saturday, July 9, the Battle of Monocacy took place at the river of that name, three miles south of the town. The Union army was defeated by a strong Confederate force, but the Union stand at the river slowed the advance toward Washington by the Southern army. Over the weekend, the troops defending the Capital were reinforced by several large units of the Union Army.

On our way from Frederick toward Bethesda we passed through Urbana, Hyattstown, Clarksburg, and Gaithersburg. The latter place got its start when, soon after 1800, Benjamin Gaither built a house on some farmland that was surveyed in 1722. This was the beginning of a settlement that remained small for several decades. After the railroad came through in the 1870s, the rate of growth increased and the town became a center of trade for the area. A few more miles brought us to Rockville. All of the towns and cities on our route southeast from Frederick were passed through by Confederate troops in early July, 1864, in their unsuccessful attempt to capture Washington.

Rockville, the county seat of Montgomery County, was called Montgomery Court House for a few years after it was settled. In 1784, Thomas Williams mapped out the town and changed the name to Williamsburg. Soon after 1800 the name became Rockville.

Gaithersburg and Rockville, along with dozens of other cities, towns, and unincorporated districts, make up the metropolitan area surrounding Washington, D.C. It is at Rockville that the author F. Scott Fitzgerald and his wife are buried.

Francis Scott Key Fitzgerald, son of Mollie and Edward Fitzgerald, was born in St. Paul, Minnesota, on September 24, 1896. His mother was born in 1860 in St. Paul and his father was born in 1853 on a farm near Rockville. One of his ancestors was the brother of Francis Scott Key, author of "The Star-Spangled Banner."

F. Scott Fitzgerald's first novel was published in 1920 and this was followed by a second novel in 1922. Many short stories were published in the following years, and in 1925 another novel, *The Great Gatsby*, was published. The author died in Hollywood, California, on December 21, 1940, at the age of 44. The last paragraph of his novel, *The Great Gatsby*, is inscribed on Francis Scott Key

18

Fitzgerald's gravestone. This is located in the cemetery that is near St. Mary's Church in Rockville.

At Bethesda, where we soon arrived, we saw the Madonna of the Trail Monument, located near the Bethesda Post Office. This is the farthest east of the twelve monuments; the one farthest west is in Upland, California.

The inscription on one panel of the base reads:

THIS, THE FIRST MILITARY ROAD
IN AMERICA
BEGINNING AT ROCK CREEK AND
POTOMAC RIVER,
GEORGETOWN, MARYLAND
LEADING OUR PIONEERS
ACROSS THIS CONTINENT
TO THE PACIFIC.

The inscription on the other panel states:

OVER THIS HIGHWAY
MARCHED THE ARMY OF
MAJOR GENERAL
EDWARD BRADDOCK
APRIL 14-1755
ON ITS WAY TO FORT DUQUESNE.

With the growth and development of Washington, D.C. as the nation's capital, Georgetown, lying west of Rock Creek, lost its identity. It became part of the city of Washington during the decade of the 1920's.

The monument here was dedicated on April 19, 1929, and was the last of the twelve to be dedicated.

Bethesda is situated between the Capital Beltway and the District of Columbia boundary. In 1940, the area was sparsely populated, with only a few hundred people. A half-century later, in 1990, the census showed that the population exceeded 62,000.

The biblical name of this Washington suburb is found in the Book of Saint John, chapter 5, verse 2:

Now there is at Jerusalem by the sheep market a pool, which is called in the Hebrew tongue Bethesda, having five porches.

The Madonna of the Trail Monument at Bethesda was not the first of these that we have seen, but it was the beginning of our planned cross-country trip to visit all of the twelve Monuments. After taking photographs of this Pioneer Mother and her children, we left Bethesda and backtracked to Frederick. We stopped here briefly, then continued toward the northwest.

At Braddock Heights, we went over Catoctin Mountain; within a few miles we reached Middletown. Many of the wounded during the Battles of South Mountain and Antietam, in 1862, were cared for in this town. Middletown was settled in the 1700s and was incorporated soon after 1830.

The countryside west of Middletown is hilly and scenic, and the highway we were following crosses over South Mountain. Partway down, after leaving the top of the mountain, a road that goes to the right leads to Washington Monument State Park.

Leaving the car in the parking area there, after a walk of several minutes up a wide trail that curves through the trees, the Monument came into view.

On July 4, 1827, a stone monument was built on this site by residents of nearby Boonsboro. It was dedicated to George Washington, leader in the War for Independence, and the first President of the United States. After more than a century, the present monument was built by the Civilian Conservation Corps, and on July 4, 1936, it was rededicated. At several places along the trail to the monument, wooden plaques, mounted on posts, tell of important events and dates in the life of George Washington.

Near this trail there is a wooden sign, supported by two posts, but this has no relationship to the historic plaques that are nearby. It is a north-south signpost for the Appalachian Trail that extends from Mount Katahdin in Maine to Springer Mountain in Georgia.

The trail enters Maryland after traversing Pennsylvania, then crosses Maryland through this area, to Weverton on the Potomac River, a few miles east of Harpers Ferry, West Virginia. From Weverton, the trail continues southward through Virginia and on to Georgia. After our visit to this Monument that is a memorial to our first President, we continued to the next town on our route.

Boonsboro, settled in 1774, grew slowly for more than fifty years, but during the 1830s the town prospered because of the increase in the number of westbound travelers. There were Civil War skirmishes in the town. After the Battle of Antietam, only a few miles away, many wounded men were cared for in Boonsboro.

The road north from Boonsboro took us through Benevola and Funkstown, originally called Jerusalem, then to Hagerstown, county seat of Washington County. In 1762, Jonathan Hager, an early settler in the area, planned this town which soon was called Hager's Town. Subsequently, the present Hagerstown emerged as the name. Jonathan Hager was born in 1719 and died in 1775, as the result of an accident. In the half-century after it was founded, the population increased to about 2,500.

West of Hagerstown, the highway follows the route of a turnpike built early in the nineteenth century, from Baltimore to Cumberland, Maryland. About 2 1/2 miles after passing through Huyett, the road crosses Conococheague Creek. Continuing west through Clear Spring and Indian Springs, the highway then closely follows the Potomac River to Hancock.

Hancock was a convenient stopping place for travelers making the trip from Baltimore to Cumberland after the turnpike was built. It is here that the distance across Maryland, from the Pennsylvania state line at the north to the West Virginia state line at the south, is only two miles. After leaving Hancock, more grades and curves are the rule as the highway goes through mountainous country. Several miles west of Hancock we entered Allegany County, then continued to Cumberland, after stopping briefly at Flintstone.

A trading post at the junction of Will's Creek and the Potomac River was established about 1750 and was named Will's Creek. Late in 1753 Major George Washington, only 21 years old, was sent by the governor of Virginia on a mission to the French. The

British government had authorized settlement in what is now Ohio. The French had built a fort near Lake Erie and were ready to move against the English settlers. Major Washington left Williamsburg, Virginia, on October 31, 1753, and on November 14 arrived at Will's Creek. With a guide and a small party he started for the Ohio Territory. It was extremely difficult to travel through the wilderness because of the severe weather, but he finally reached the French outpost. Here he delivered the letter from the Virginia governor that warned the French to pull back their forces, but they refused to comply with the governor's demands. George Washington had failed to stop the forces of France, but the publication of his journal in January, 1754, after his return to Williamsburg, publicized the French threat.

In 1755 the Will's Creek trading post was fortified and the name was changed to Fort Cumberland. Thirty years later, Washington Town was established at this site, and in 1787 the name was changed to Cumberland. In 1789 Cumberland became the county seat of Allegany County.

By the early years of the nineteenth century the country lying north and west of the Ohio River was being settled. After much debate the Congress of the United States authorized funds in 1806 for "laying out and making a road from Cumberland, in the state of Maryland, to the state of Ohio." President Thomas Jefferson signed the Act of Congress on March 29, 1806. Construction of the Cumberland Road, also called the National Road or National Pike, started in 1811 and was completed to Wheeling, in the western section of Virginia, in 1818. In the latter year, mail coaches were running from Washington, D.C. to Wheeling.

As soon as we arrived in Cumberland we went to the Tourism Office in the Western Maryland Railroad Depot. Here they were helpful in giving directions and we soon found that Riverside Park, at the junction of Will's Creek and the Potomac River, is within walking distance of the Depot. George Washington's Headquarters, a one-room cabin, is located in Riverside Park. This was built in the 1750s for Washington's use, and was available at any time he was at Fort Cumberland. Originally located in the fort, the cabin was restored to its original condition and moved to its present location in 1921. It is the only building of Fort Cumberland that remains after more than two centuries.

Leaving Cumberland, with its elevation between 600 feet and 700 feet above sea level, we went through La Vale and Clarysville. Within ten miles the highway climbed more than 1,000 feet through the mountains as we reached Eckhart Mines at an elevation of 1,720 feet.

Continuing west we soon came to Frostburg with its highway sign, "WELCOME TO FRIENDLY FROSTBURG." This town had its start in 1812 when Meshach Frost built a tavern on the National Road. He called the settlement that took root around the tavern, Mount Pleasant, but soon it was referred to as Frost's Town. Several years later it officially became Frostburg. It is the home of Frostburg State University, founded in 1898. In the beginning this was a two-year state normal school.

From an elevation of just over 1,900 feet at Frostburg the highway ascends to 2,800 feet as it enters Garrett County. This county was established in 1872 and was named for John Work Garrett, president of the Baltimore and Ohio Railroad. John W. Garrett was born on July 31, 1820, and his death occurred on September 26, 1884.

Several miles after entering Garrett County, the road drops about 500 feet into a valley. Here it crosses the Casselman River before reaching Grantsville with its informative "WELCOME TO GRANTSVILLE" sign. Named for Daniel Grant, this town was started before 1800. The highway then goes over its highest point in Maryland, less than four miles west of Grantsville, and soon crosses the summit of Keyser's Ridge before reaching the Pennsylvania state line.

We were always on the lookout for descriptive signs along the highway, and at some point near here, before we arrived at the state boundary, we saw this road sign, "Pig's Ear Road." Our trip across Maryland, started east of Chesapeake Bay, was completed as we entered Pennsylvania.

Chapter 3

Pennsylvania

As we entered the Keystone State we were greeted by a message on a large sign:

WELCOME TO PENNSYLVANIA
America Starts Here
Robert P. Casey, Governor

When we crossed the state boundary, we were in Somerset County and soon arrived at Addison, whose Main Street is signed "National Road." Only a few miles farther along we crossed Youghiogheny River Lake over a fairly long bridge. The countryside here is at a lower elevation than the mountainous area we had traveled through east of Keyser's Ridge. The Youghiogheny River Lake at the bridge is at an elevation of about 1,400 feet. From there we continued northwest and at about twelve miles from the river came to Fort Necessity National Battlefield.

After George Washington returned to Williamsburg, Virginia, in early 1754 from his mission to warn the French in Ohio, his stay there was brief. In April, having been promoted to lieutenant colonel, he returned to Will's Creek in command of a contingent of Virginia troops, then continued west into present-day Pennsylvania. On May 28, 1754, a detachment led by Washington caught by surprise a party of Frenchmen commanded by Coulon de Jumonville. In a skirmish lasting about fifteen minutes, several of the French, including Jumonville, were killed, and only one of Washington's party was a fatality in the battle.

During June a palisade fort was built at the present site of Fort Necessity. Late in the month Colonel Washington received alarming information about the movement of French and Indian forces. He ordered his troops to prepare for the defense of the fort. On July 3, Fort Necessity was attacked by a large force of French and

Indians. The garrison of the fort was heavily outnumbered and was forced to surrender. The terms proposed by the French commander and accepted by Colonel Washington allowed the Colonial troops to withdraw with honors of war. On July 4, 1754, 22 years before the Declaration of Independence was signed, Colonel Washington led his troops away from Fort Necessity and back to Will's Creek. This early triumph of France in the French and Indian War was followed by a greater victory the following year.

After losing Fort Necessity the British government made a decision to confront France seriously in North America. In early 1755 Major General Edward Braddock arrived in Virginia, along with more than 1,000 trained British troops. He was appointed as commander in chief of all British forces in the American colonies. On March 15, 1755, an army made up of regular troops and American militia left Alexandria, Virginia, for Fort Cumberland. The general was impatient to move against the French, but he had no idea of the lack of roads through the American wilderness, nor of the weather conditions that existed in late winter or early spring.

Finally, in May, 1755, the vanguard of Braddock's army left Fort Cumberland. It was necessary to cut a road through the mountains for the army supply wagons, and the slow progress of the British army gave the French plenty of time to prepare for battle. General Braddock was confident that with his army of 2,000 men he could capture Fort Duquesne. This was the French headquarters that in later years would become Pittsburgh.

In order to move more rapidly toward the fort, the general pushed ahead with more than 1,400 of his troops. The remainder of the army was to follow with the heavy equipment as soon as possible. On July 9, 1755, at a point about eight miles from Fort Duquesne, the French soldiers and their several hundred Indian allies were hidden in the thick underbrush, waiting for the oncoming army. At a signal, they fired at close range on the advancing troops. General Braddock, accustomed to fighting a battle in which his troops were in disciplined ranks, had little knowledge of frontier fighting. The French and Indians, firing from behind trees and in ravines, completely routed the English army in the two hour Battle of the Monongahela. British casualties were extremely heavy and General Braddock was seriously wounded. George Washington, on the General's staff, was uninjured but narrowly escaped when bullets went through his clothes. The British general was carried by the retreating soldiers as they made their way toward Fort Cumberland. On July 13, 1755, he died about a mile from Fort Necessity.

The experience gained by George Washington during the French and Indian War prepared him for the American Revolution two decades later. In his early twenties he showed great ability as a military leader and was well prepared to take command of the Continental Army in 1775.

Fort Necessity National Battlefield preserves a segment of our history that occurred before the Revolutionary War. We found it very interesting. The battlefield has been administered by the National Park Service since 1933. In 1962 additional land was incorporated into the national battlefield, including the site of General Braddock's grave. Besides a slide presentation, the Visitor Center has exhibits that tell the story of the battle and the defense of the fort, by means of photographs, maps, and drawings. The Mount Washington Tavern is only a few hundred yards from the Visitor Center. This tavern was built on the National Road in 1818 by Nathaniel Ewing, and became a well-known stage stop. The restored tavern is now a museum and is administered as part of the Fort Necessity National Battlefield.

While we were in the Visitor Center we noticed a counted cross-stitch kit with directions for making a picture of the Mount Washington Tavern. This is the type of needlework that G enjoyed, and we purchased the kit. (Note: For a long time, to save extra writing, we have often used our initials, G or V, instead of writing our first names.) After completing our coast-to-coast trip, she finished the picture. It is framed, and hangs on the living room wall of our home.

We continued to the northwest after we left the battlefield and went through Chalk Hill, as the highway continued its climb to the crest of Chestnut Ridge at an elevation of more than 2,400 feet. In the next three miles the road descends to the town of Hopwood, started in 1791 by John Hopwood. Originally called Woodstock, the name was changed later to Monroe for our fifth president, James Monroe. For many years, it has been Hopwood, the name of its founder. When the National Road was in its heyday, several taverns here made this town a popular place for those traveling by stagecoach.

From Hopwood it is a short distance to Uniontown, the county seat of Fayette County. In July, 1776, Henry Beeson established Uniontown, which he first referred to as Beeson's Town. We had been traveling through Fayette County since we crossed the Youghiogheny River Lake, a distance of more than twenty miles. This county was formed on September 26, 1783, by an act of the legislature; its name honored the Marquis de Lafayette. In 1777 this young member of the French nobility became a major general in the American army and served on the staff of General George Washington. Within a few months he was placed in command of an infantry division. From that time until the end of the war he aided the American cause, not only as a leader on the battlefield, but because of his influence in obtaining more military support from France. Many counties and cities in the United States have been named Lafayette after this French nobleman, and others have been named Fayette by omitting the first two letters of the name.

George C. Marshall was born in Uniontown on December 31, 1880, and during his boyhood years in western Pennsylvania he learned of George Washington's early military deeds. Marshall's United States Army career began as a second lieutenant in 1902 after his graduation from Virginia Military Institute. During his long military life as a professional soldier, his tours of duty included service in the Philippines, in France (during World War I), in China for three years (1924-1927), and he also had many stateside assignments. His promotion to brigadier general came in 1936, and in 1944, during World War II, he became General of the Army.

After his resignation as Chief of Staff in November, 1945, he was on a mission to China, then was appointed Secretary of State in the Truman administration, in January, 1947. Five months after he became Secretary of State, George C. Marshall, in a speech on June 5, 1947, announced a program to aid the countries of Europe in their rebuilding after the destruction that took place in World War II. This soon was known as the Marshall Plan.

This outstanding American was awarded the Nobel Peace Prize in 1953. George C. Marshall died in Washington, D.C. on October 16, 1959.

We drove on to the northwest and soon we were in Brownsville. The earliest name of this town was Redstone Old Fort from a nearby Indian mound. Thomas Brown was an early inhabitant of the area and drew up the plans for the layout of Brownsville in 1785.

Philander C. Knox was born here on May 6, 1853. He attended Mount Union College in Alliance, Ohio, and after graduating returned to Pennsylvania. Knox practiced law in Pittsburgh for more than twenty years, and, in 1901, became attorney general of the United States in the cabinet of President William McKinley. After President McKinley was assassinated in Buffalo, New York, in September, 1901, Knox remained as attorney general under President Theodore Roosevelt until 1904. In that year he was appointed as U.S. Senator from Pennsylvania, and later was elected to return to the Senate. President William Howard Taft appointed Knox Secretary of State in 1909. He served until 1913, then returned to Pittsburgh and resumed his law practice. In 1916 he was again elected to the Senate of the United States and represented the people of Pennsylvania until his death on October 12, 1921.

As we left Brownsville we crossed the Monongahela River and entered West Brownsville in Washington County. This county was established by the legislature on March 28, 1781. West Brownsville was mapped out by Ephraim L. Blaine in 1831, nearly fifty years after neighboring Brownsville was founded.

In the years following the French and Indian War a few settlers came to western Pennsylvania, but after the American Revolution, population growth increased. Many towns were founded and farming became an important part of the region's economy.

During the Revolution a small excise tax on whiskey was put into effect, but for a few years, little was done to collect the tax. Early in 1791, during the first administration of President George Washington, an excise tax on whiskey was levied. Farmers in western Pennsylvania were many miles from a market for their grain.

For several years they had resorted to distilling part of their grain into whiskey which could be more economically shipped to the eastern market. The tax raised the price of the whiskey and reduced or eliminated any profit they might make. Revenue collectors were sent to collect the tax but many times they were driven away or were manhandled by the irate farmers.

By the summer of 1794, the Whiskey Rebellion, sometimes called the Whiskey Insurrection, was in full swing in four counties of western Pennsylvania: Washington, Fayette, Allegheny, and Westmoreland. In mid-July, there was armed confrontation between the rebellious farmers and a group of soldiers defending a general's house. This resulted in the death of one of the insurgents and the wounding of several on both sides. A few days after this battle, hundreds of people, including several local officials, met to make plans for a general insurrection in the region.

Before the end of July, a sizable army had been organized and, on August 1, 1794, this army camped near Pittsburgh. The next day, they entered the town with the intention of destroying it, but after burning one or two buildings, they marched out of the town without doing more damage.

Early in August, 1794, President Washington issued a proclamation. He ordered all of those taking part in the rebellion to return to their homes, and sent an army of about 15,000 troops to western Pennsylvania.

This army was led by officers who had served under General Washington during the American Revolution. When the militia troops arrived in western Pennsylvania the rebellion soon collapsed and in November, 1794, raids were conducted that resulted in the capture of most of the leaders. A number of these men were put on trial, and two were found guilty and sentenced to be hanged but received pardons from President Washington.

The decision made by our first president to crush the Whiskey Rebellion confirmed the authority of the newly established government of the Unites Staes to deal with such a crisis.

James Gillespie Blaine, son of Ephraim Lyon Blaine, was born in West Brownsville on January 31, 1830. He graduated from Washington College (now Washington and Jefferson College) in

1847, then taught school. During the years that he was teaching he furthered his education by studying law; then in the early 1850s he moved to Augusta, Maine. In 1858, he was elected to the state legislature of Maine and served four years, 1859 through 1862.

James G. Blaine represented Maine in the United States House of Representatives from 1863 to 1876. He was a Republican and held the office of Speaker of the House from 1869 to 1876. Following this he was elected to the U.S. Senate, where he served until 1881, when he was appointed Secretary of State in the cabinet of President James A. Garfield. After President Garfield's death on September 19, 1881, from an assassin's bullet, Blaine remained as Secretary of State under President Chester A. Arthur for a short time until his replacement was named later in 1881. In 1884, Blaine ran for president on the Republican ticket and lost to Grover Cleveland in a very close election. His last years of government service were spent as Secretary of State from 1889 to 1892 in the administration of President Benjamin Harrison. James G. Blaine died in Washington, D.C. on January 27, 1893.

The Madonna of the Trail Monument in Pennsylvania is located at the town of Beallsville in Washington County, on the highway from Uniontown to Washington. This is the second of the twelve Madonna Monuments that commemorate The National Old Trails Road. Dedicated on Saturday, December 8, 1928, it is located on the route laid out by Thomas Cresap, from Will's Creek (Cumberland) Maryland to the Monongahela River at the mouth of Redstone Creek. In 1751 Cresap had cleared a narrow track or road from Will's Creek to the forks of the Youghiogheny River. During the spring or summer of 1752 he was given the job of extending this road to the Monongahela, and Cresap asked Nemacolin, a Delaware Indian, to help him.

This road-building project was very difficult because they lacked proper equipment and materials. When completed, the road was only a trail marked with tree blazes and rock cairns. It became known as Nemacolin's Path or Nemacolin's Trail and was the route followed by Lieutenant Colonel George Washington in May, 1754, and a year later by General Braddock when he met the French and

Indians with such disastrous results. In later years the main highway through this area closely followed this trail.

One of the inscriptions on the Madonna of the Trail Monument at Beallsville is as follows:

ON THIS HISTORIC SPOT
THE HUNTING GROUND
OF THE FRIENDLY INDIAN
NEMACOLIN
THIS MONUMENT
IS ERECTED AND DEDICATED
TO THE MEMORY OF OUR
PIONEER MOTHERS

The other inscription:

ERECTED IN
NINETEEN HUNDRED TWENTY EIGHT
IN WASHINGTON COUNTY
PENNSYLVANIA
THE OLDEST COUNTY WEST OF
THE ALLEGHENY MOUNTAINS
NAMED FOR THE FATHER
OF OUR COUNTRY

A plaque placed at the base of the Monument gives this information:

MADONNA OF THE TRAIL
Presented and dedicated
December 8, 1928
By the
National Society of the
Daughters of the American Revolution
Restored 1990 by the
Pennsylvania State Society
Daughters of the American Revolution
Mrs. Thomas G. Burkey, State Regent
Rededicated June 23, 1990

32

We continued on to Washington, with its entrance sign, "WEL-COME TO WASHINGTON, PA— HOME OF PONY BASE-BALL." The town of Washington was founded by David Hoge in 1781, the year that the county was formed, and soon was made the county seat of the new county. Hoge laid out the town on land originally occupied by an Indian village called Catfish Camp. He named it "Bassett Town," but before year-end in 1781, Washington became the name.

Washington and Jefferson College, in Washington, has a history dating back to the year the county and town were founded. A sign mounted between two posts states, "WASHINGTON and JEFFERSON COLLEGE founded 1781." On March 4, 1865, the merger of Washington College and Jefferson College of nearby Canonsburg took place.

In 1922, the Washington and Jefferson College football team played in the Rose Bowl at Pasadena, California. The opposing team was the University of California and the game ended with a scoreless tie, 0-0.

Ten miles beyond Washington brought us to Claysville, founded in 1832, as shown on the highway sign. This town on the National Road was named for Henry Clay who was instrumental in passing the legislation by Congress that authorized the use of federal funds to build this road. Clay traveled over the National Road many times in going from his home in Kentucky to the national capital.

On a farm a few miles south of Claysville in the southwestern corner of Washington County, William Holmes McGuffey was born September 23, 1800. In the latter part of 1802, when he was two years old, his parents moved to Ohio where they lived in a log cabin near Youngstown, in Mahoning County. As a boy, McGuffey grew up under frontier conditions but his early schooling prepared him to enter college. When he was eighteen years old he entered Washington College in Washington, Pennsylvania, the college nearest his home. To finance his education he taught school, and it was while he was teaching at Paris, Kentucky, about two years before his graduation, that he met Dr. Robert H. Bishop.

Dr. Bishop became the first president of Miami University at Oxford, Ohio, on March 30, 1825. After William Holmes McGuffey graduated in 1826 he was appointed professor of Ancient Languages at Miami, and, along with two other professors and four tutors, assisted Dr. Bishop in operating the university in its early days.

In August, 1836, Dr. McGuffey left Miami University and became the president of Cincinnati College, a position he held until 1839. He held other positions as a college professor until July 28, 1845, when he moved to Charlottesville, Virginia. Here he served as a professor at the University of Virginia for many years.

While he was teaching at Miami University, he wrote the manuscripts for the *First* and *Second McGuffey Readers*. These were published in 1836, the year he went to Cincinnati. In 1837, the *Third* and *Fourth Readers* were published and W. H. McGuffey was assisted in compiling these by his younger brother, Alexander. Publications of the *Fifth* and *Sixth McGuffey Readers* occurred several years after the first four *Readers* were published. Printing of various revised editions of the McGuffey school books continued for many years, from the late 1830s to the 1920s.

Generations of school children studied the *McGuffey Readers* and millions of books were printed and used in schools.

William Holmes McGuffey died May 4, 1873, at Charlottesville, Virginia. This man who devoted his life to furthering the education of young Americans has not been forgotten by the people of western Washington County where he was born. We passed the McGuffey High School and Middle School, situated near Claysville, and, a few miles farther along, near West Alexander, we noted West Alexander School — McGuffey School District.

West Alexander was established in 1796 by Robert Humphrey, a veteran of the Revolutionary War. The town is situated on higher ground and overlooks part of the West Virginia Panhandle.

Our trip through southwestern Pennsylvania ended just beyond West Alexander as we entered West Virginia.

Chapter 4

West Virginia

A glance at the map of West Virginia shows a strip of land between Ohio and Pennsylvania that resembles a wedge driven between the two states, east of the Ohio River. This Panhandle, usually called the Northern Panhandle, came about after the western boundary of Pennsylvania was finally determined in 1785. The boundary line between Maryland and Pennsylvania was a source of dispute between the two states from the earliest days of settlement. The same can be said of the boundary between Virginia and Pennsylvania, farther west. The dispute had its origin in the seventeenth century when charters were issued by the King of England without accurate information concerning the geography of the area that he granted. The result was that the charter of Maryland issued in 1632 and the grant given to William Penn in 1681 contained some of the same territory.

In August, 1763, two men who were distinguished mathematicians and astronomers, were named as surveyors to determine the correct boundary. They were Charles Mason and Jeremiah Dixon, from London, England. The starting point of the boundary is at the northeast corner of Maryland, a few miles west of the Delaware River. The cornerstone of the Mason-Dixon Line was planted there in a deep ravine, late in 1764, and the boundary line between Pennsylvania and Maryland runs due west from that point.

Besides Mason and Dixon and their assistants, the survey project required a small army of workers. These included chain carriers, axemen, cooks, baggage carriers, and a number of other workers to perform various tasks as required. In 1765 and 1766 the work progressed steadily except during the winter months, and by October, 1767, the line had been extended to a point several miles west of the Monongahela River.

The Indians of the area had remained peaceful but the tribal chiefs held a council and the surveyors were told that the work must stop, and that the line could not go farther west. Charles Mason and Jeremiah Dixon returned to the east, and, late in December, 1767, were paid the balance due them and given an honorable discharge.

Nothing was done about the boundary for more than fifteen years after the Indians stopped the Mason-Dixon survey. By 1784 the area was being settled and the Indians were no longer a threat. In that year the line was continued to the west, and the southwestern corner of Pennsylvania was determined accurately and marked with an oak post surrounded with a pile of stones. In 1785 the western boundary of the state was surveyed from the southwestern corner north to the Ohio River. In 1786 the line was completed north to Lake Erie.

The Mason-Dixon Line established the boundary between Pennsylvania and Maryland as the authorities of the two states had planned. Later, when the line was extended west between Pennsylvania and present-day West Virginia, the boundary between those states were also established. Because the meandering Potomac River sets the southern boundary of Maryland for many miles, western Maryland was "compressed" between the river and the Mason-Dixon Line. As we noted at Hancock, the state is two miles wide at that point.

When a line was surveyed straight west from the southwestern corner of Pennsylvania, to all intents an extension of the Mason-Dixon Line, it became the southern boundary of the West Virginia Northern Panhandle. Four counties lie north of this line, and from the north they are Hancock, 83 square miles; Brooke, 89 square miles; Ohio, 106 square miles; and Marshall, 307 square miles.

Soon after we entered West Virginia we came to a State of West Virginia metal plaque mounted on a pole. It stated:

OHIO COUNTY

Formed in 1776 from West Augusta. Named for the River which bears an Indian name meaning "Beautiful River." Scene of last battle of the Revolution, 1782. Visited by La Salle, Celeron, Gist, Washington, and later explorers.

36

A little farther along we came to a white milepost in the shape of an obelisk. On one surface is inscribed:

120
to
Cumberland
to
W. Alexander
4 1/2

On the adjoining surface:

11
to
WHEELING
to
Triadelphia
3 1/2

We drove through Valley Grove and at Roney's Point, about five miles west of the state line, there is another State of West Virginia plaque:

RONEY'S POINT
Here is located the historic "Heimberger House,"
one of the first and most famous of the numerous
stopping places which sprang up to serve the traffic on the National Road. Still standing, it is now
called the "Old Stone House."

This Roney's Point plaque stands across the highway from the building, marked in large letters, STONE HOUSE. A covered veranda with a railing extends along one side of the house.

Just over a mile west of Roney's Point, another State plaque commemorates Triadelphia:

TRIADELPHIA
Named for three friends. Near this spot, on Middle
Wheeling Creek, Jonathan Link built a blockhouse
in 1780. Next year a band of 20 Indians killed Link
and two companions, and captured and toma-
hawked Presley Peak and William Hawkins.

This town was an important stagecoach stop in the early days
of the National Road, and was incorporated in 1829.

We soon reached Wheeling, "THE FRIENDLY CITY," as pro-
claimed by a sign. In 1769, the pioneer, Ebenezer Zane (born October 7, 1747, died November 19, 1812) established his claim to
land at the present site of Wheeling. During 1770 he built a log
cabin there and named the new settlement Zanesburg. In 1774 Fort
Fincastle was built near the small colony which by this time was
referred to as Wheeling. Two years later, early in the American
Revolution, the name of the fort was changed from Fort Fincastle
to Fort Henry, and, in that year, Wheeling became the official name
of the town.

During three days in 1782, September 11, 12 and 13, the last
battle of the Revolution was fought at Wheeling when Fort Henry
was attacked by a contingent of British troops and nearly 300 Indians. The defenders of the fort were able to withstand the lengthy
battle that occurred nearly eleven months after the British surrendered at Yorktown, Virginia, on October 19, 1781

In 1793, more than twenty years after Zane built his log cabin
at the site of Wheeling, he mapped out more than 100 lots that
became the nucleus of the growing town, and in 1794 a post office
was in operation. By 1806, when a charter was issued, traffic and
commerce on the Ohio River were bringing prosperity to the area.
More than a decade later the National Road reached the town, and
two highway signs, similar to those previously mentioned, give
facts about this road.

THE NATIONAL PIKE
The National Pike, called the "Old Cumberland
Road," was started in 1811 and used to Wheeling

38

in 1817 and by mail coaches from Washington by 1818. Most of it followed the Nemacolin Path and Braddock's Road from Cumberland, Md.

—

ELM GROVE STONE BRIDGE
Built in 1817 by Moses Shepherd, a prominent Ohio Countian, as part of the National Road. Constructed of uncoursed limestone, but covered by concrete in 1958, it is the oldest extant three span elliptical arch bridge in the state. Also know as "Monument Place Bridge" due to the nearby memorial built to Henry Clay by Shepherd in honor of his support for National Road construction.

In the years after the completion of this road to Wheeling, thousands of people came through on their way to settle the Ohio River Valley and the adjoining country. It became an important transfer point for the untold tons of merchandise and the many sheep, cattle, and hogs that arrived by way of the National Road and on the Ohio River.

Wheeling was incorporated as a city in 1836, and during the years that followed, it became an important manufacturing center. After the railroad was built from Cumberland, Maryland, the first passenger train reached Wheeling in January, 1853.

On December 20, 1860, the state of South Carolina voted to secede from the Union. A few months later the Civil War opened when Confederate forces shelled Fort Sumter in the harbor of Charleston, South Carolina, on April 12, 1861. Five days later the Virignia convention voted to secede, but popular sentiment in the western counties of the state was against leaving the Union. Delegates from these counties met at Wheeling on May 13, 1861, and during the convention voted against secession. From June 19, 1861, to June 20, 1863, Wheeling was the capital of the government that was set up by the 26 counties. On the latter date, West Virginia was admitted to the Union and Wheeling became the first capital of the new state.

After nearly seven years, the state capital was moved to Charleston on April 1, 1870, and it remained there until it was returned to Wheeling on May 23, 1875. Charleston became the capital again on May 1, 1885, and has remained the state capital of West Virginia since that date.

The third Madonna of the Trail Monument is located at the entrance to Wheeling Municipal Park. This monument was dedicated Saturday, July 7, 1928.

Inscribed on one side is this fitting tribute:

TO THE PIONEER MOTHERS
OF OUR MOUNTAIN STATE
WHOSE COURAGE, OPTIMISM, LOVE
AND SACRIFICE MADE POSSIBLE
THE NATIONAL HIGHWAY
THAT UNITED THE EAST AND WEST

The inscription on the other side reads:

BY THE AUTHORITY OF THE
UNITED STATES GOVERNMENT
AND CHIEFLY THROUGH
THE STATESMANSHIP OF
HENRY CLAY
THIS ROAD WAS MADE POSSIBLE
IN 1806

It has been more than two centuries since the young pioneer, Ebenezer Zane, built his log cabin where Wheeling is located. From this beginning, Wheeling has become a well-known city on the Ohio River, with a 1990 Census population of 34,882.

Our trip through West Virginia was limited to about sixteen miles, since our route took us across the Panhandle. We then went over the Ohio River bridge and entered Ohio at Bridgeport.

Chapter 5

Ohio

Bridgeport was founded by Ebenezer Zane in 1806; he named it Canton. This occurred more than a third of a century after he built the first log cabin at the site of Wheeling. Beyond Bridgeport we went through Brookside, then, after a few miles came to St. Clairsville.

By the 1780s, as the American Revolution came to an end, thousands of settlers had pushed across the Appalachian Mountains into the present states of Kentucky, Tennessee, and Ohio. The first two of these states were sufficiently populated to be admitted to the Union in 1792 and 1796. The Continental Congress, on July 13, 1787, adopted the "Ordinance for the Government of the Territory of the United States Northwest of the River Ohio." This is known as the Ordinance of 1787.

On October 5, 1787, General Arthur St. Clair was appointed governor of the territory, an area that eventually would be divided into five states of the United States.

Arthur St. Clair was born in Scotland in 1734. In 1757, he entered the British military service and was sent to North America. He served in Canada during the French and Indian War and was an officer under General James Wolfe in the Battle on the Plains of Abraham that resulted in the defeat of the French who were defending Quebec. In the American Revolution General St. Clair served with Commander in Chief George Washington and had a part in the American victory at Trenton, New Jersey, in December, 1776. This was followed early in 1777 by the defeat of the British at Princeton.

In 1785, Fort Harmar was built at the confluence of the Muskingum River and the Ohio River. Three years later, in April, 1788, settlers arrived at the fort. Within a few weeks, Marietta, the first town in Ohio, had its start. Governor St. Clair arrived at Marietta on July 9, 1788, to begin his duties, and on July 27, one of his first official acts was to establish Washington County, the first county in the territory. At the time it was created, this county covered more than a third of the present state and extended far north of the Ohio River.

After Washington County was laid out and as the population of the Northwest Territory increased, there was a need for roads leading to the western country. In 1796, Ebenezer Zane was given a contract by Congress to open a trace or road west of Wheeling. Most of the work was done in 1796 and 1797, and the project was finished in 1798. The route that Zane laid out went westerly from a point across the Ohio River from Wheeling, then through what is now St. Clairsville, to Cambridge and Zanesville. Here he turned to the southwest through Lancaster and Chillicothe to Aberdeen on the Ohio River, across from Maysville (then called Limestone), Kentucky.

Zane's Trace was the first road west and north of the Ohio River. It had little resemblance to a road as we know it. Trees and underbrush were cleared away, some low spots were filled with tree branches, there were fords where it was possible to cross the smaller streams, and ferries were available at the rivers. When the trace was completed it was a trail or rough path through the wilderness, wide enough for a person on horseback. Soon after it was completed, wagon traffic began to widen it, and, in time, it became a highway.

When we crossed the river at Bridgeport we entered Belmont County, one of the oldest of Ohio's 88 counties. Leaving the Ohio River the highway rises quickly into the hills that are characteristic of this section of Ohio. Belmont, the name of the county, is of French origin, meaning, "beautiful mountain" or "fine mountain," in reference to this hilly county. It was established by Governor St. Clair on September 7, 1801, and was the ninth county that was set up in the Northwest Territory. The area was originally part of Washington County, created by the governor in 1788. In 1797, St. Clair had laid out Jefferson County by making it from part of the northern portion of Washington County. Following this, in 1801, he took part of Jefferson County to form Belmont County. St. Clairsville, named for General St. Clair, was made the county seat in 1803.

One provision of the Ordinance of 1787 stipulated that when a proposed state had 60,000 inhabitants it could be admitted into the Union. The census of 1800 reported more than 45,000 inhabitants in Ohio and the population was increasing rapidly. On March 1, 1803, Ohio became the seventeenth state, with Edward Tiffin as governor and Chillicothe as the first state capital.

As we have seen, the Cumberland Road was carrying traffic from the east to Wheeling in 1818. For the next several years the federal government wrestled with the constitutional question as to whether to extend the road to the west. The population of Ohio had increased steadily during these years. Indiana had entered the Union in 1816, and Illinois in 1818. In 1820, Congress appropriated money for a survey of the road from Wheeling to a point on the east bank of the Mississippi River near St. Louis.

The important breakthrough for proponents of the road came on March 3, 1825, when an act was passed that set aside money to build the National Road from the west bank of the Ohio River, across from Wheeling, to Zanesville, Ohio. Also in the act was money to extend the survey for the National Road to the capital of Missouri.

July 4, 1825, was a special day for the people of St. Clairsville and the surrounding country, besides being Independence Day. On this holiday, after a delay of seven years, ground was broken at St. Clairsville for the extension of the National Road westward in Ohio.

We continued west from St. Clairsville through Morristown, and several miles farther along we entered Guernsey County. Early in the nineteenth century, a number of settlers came here from the Island of Guernsey in the English Channel, and this county was named for their homeland. It was formed March 1, 1810, from parts of Belmont and Muskingum counties. The soil of this county and some nearby areas was favorable for the growth of the herb, pennyroyal. During part of the nineteenth century, stills were widely used for production of the aromatic oil of this herb, and, on a smaller scale, oil was produced in the present century. The pungent mint, peppermint, was also raised for the production of peppermint oil.

The oils of pennyroyal and peppermint were important items of medicine for pioneer families living in rural areas where there were no doctors available. An abandoned house in Fairview, west of Hendrysburg, is still plainly marked with a sign — "PENNY-ROYAL — Home & Museum."

A sign, shaped like the map of Ohio, announces that the motorist is entering "OLD WASHINGTON — Site of Skirmish with General John H. Morgan's Confederate Raiders."

Ohio was heavily involved in the Civil War, sending thousands of men to the Union forces. The factories of the state produced military equipment and supplies, and farms furnished foodstuffs for the war effort. Ohioans experienced combat only once in their home state and this occurred about midway through the war.

On July 7, 1863, nearly a week after the Battle of Gettysburg, in Pennsylvania, began, General John Morgan led a force of about 2,500 Confederate cavalrymen north through Kentucky to the Ohio River. The next day he crossed the river with his troops at Brandenburg, Kentucky, moved eastward through southern Indiana, north of the Ohio River, and entered Ohio just west of Cincinnati on July 13.

Morgan's troops avoided Cincinnati and Hamilton and traveled east through the open country. The horses were fed from stocks of grain and hay on the farms, and food was demanded at farm homes and in the small towns that they passed through. Morgan led his troops into Meigs County and attempted to cross over the Ohio River at Buffington Island. He was stopped by Union gunboats and trapped by Union troops and Ohio militia forces, and a battle took place here about ten days after Morgan's Confederate cavalry entered Indiana. There were casualties on both sides, and seven hundred of Morgan's men surrendered, but General Morgan escaped with nearly 1,200 of his original force.

Two more crossing attempts were made farther up the Ohio River but neither succeeded and Morgan turned northeastward with his remaining troops. It was during this flight of the southern forces that the skirmish at Old Washington occurred, with a number of Union and Confederate men killed.

On July 26, 1863, at Salineville in Columbiana County, the final fight of this Confederate invasion of Ohio took place. The southern troops were defeated, and those who survived the battle

44

fled to the north. Later that same day, Morgan and the last of his troops were captured near Lisbon, the county seat of Columbiana County. The Confederate raid into Ohio ended at a point farther north than General Lee was able to advance into Pennsylvania earlier that month.

The last incident of General John Morgan's raid into Ohio occurred later in the year. Several weeks after he was captured, Morgan was taken to the penitentiary in Columbus. On November 27, 1863, the general and six of his officers were able to escape and Morgan made his way back to Kentucky.

Several miles west of Old Washington brought us to the city of Cambridge, county seat of Guernsey County. This city was mapped out in June, 1806, by Jacob Gomber and Zacheus Beatty. Twenty years later the National Road reached Cambridge, bringing a measure of prosperity to the community. Glass manufacturing and distribution have been important to the local economy for decades, and there are several glass factories and museums in the immediate area. John H. Glenn, one of America's early astronauts, was born here on July 18, 1921.

As mentioned in previous pages, our travel through eastern Ohio has taken us through Belmont County, a name of French origin, and through Guernsey County, named by pioneers for their homeland in the English Channel. Now we have entered Muskingum County, a name derived from the dialect of the Delaware Indians. The county was established March 1, 1804, and was formed from parts of the original Washington and Fairfield counties.

After construction of the National Road through Ohio began in 1825, the route was surveyed through Cambridge and to Zanesville. Jonathan Knight, United States Commissioner, arrived in Columbus on October 5, 1825, along with his assistants, after completing the survey from Zanesville.

In 1827 the town of Concord was laid out by David Findley near the new road. A few families that had previously set up living quarters along Zane's Trace, only two miles away, moved to Concord after Findley finished his work. The name was changed to New Concord at a later date, and Muskingum College was founded here in 1837.

William Rainey Harper, born at New Concord on July 26, 1856, attended Muskingum College and graduated while quite young, in 1870. In the next twenty years he taught at several colleges, and, in 1885, began lecturing at chautauquas during the summers. The University of Chicago was founded in 1891, and at the age of 35, Harper became its first president. William Rainey Harper died at Chicago, Illinois, on January 10, 1906.

John H. Glenn, born in nearby Cambridge, as noted earlier, is another outstanding graduate of Muskingum College, where he graduated in 1939. He served in the U.S. Marine Corps from 1942 to 1965. His career as an astronaut began in 1959, and in February, 1962, Lt. Col. Glenn became the first American to orbit the earth. Since December, 1974, John Glenn has been United States Senator from Ohio, and was reelected in 1992 for a six-year term.

Near New Concord we saw our first S-Bridge. If any are still standing east of here we failed to see them. This bridge is near the main highway which was built to bypass it, and is in very good condition.

The village of Norwich is situated a few miles west of New Concord. A small stone monument is located by the side of the main street of this village, at a point where the street goes uphill and curves to the right. The following is inscribed on this monument:

IN MEMORY
of Christopher C. Baldwin, Librarian
of The American Antiquarian Society,
Worcester, Mass., killed on this curve
Aug. 20, 1835, by the overturning of a
stagecoach. This being the first traffic
accident on record in this state.
This tablet erected by the Norwich Troop
No. 20, Boy Scouts of America.
Rollin A. Allen, Scoutmaster, 1925

The NATIONAL ROAD/ZANE GREY MUSEUM, operated under the auspices of the Ohio Historical Society, is located near

Norwich, and is about ten miles east of Zanesville. It was opened in 1973. There is a diorama of the National Road, and there are exhibits pertaining to its history, including an authentic Conestoga wagon. Zane Grey memorabilia are featured in one section of the museum.

Zane Grey, born in Zanesville on January 31, 1872, was a descendant of Ebenezer Zane. His father was a dentist, and the son studied dentistry at the University of Pennsylvania. He established a dental practice, but gave up dentistry in order to write. Zane Grey had difficulty in finding a publisher for his first books, but, beginning in his thirties, his novels began to sell. During the following years he wrote dozens of Westerns, and many of them were best sellers. Zane Grey died on October 23, 1939, at Altadena, California.

The contract by Congress in 1796 was the authority for granting Ebenezer Zane three sections of land if he completed Zane's Trace as he proposed. In 1800, about two years after the Trace was finished, he received payment from Congress for his work. He was given the three sections and had his choice of locations. Prior to receiving title that year, he had sold the 640-acre site at the junction of the Licking and Muskingum Rivers to his brother, Jonathan Zane, and to his son-in-law, John McIntire. In 1799, the town of Westbourne was founded by these relatives of Ebenezer Zane, and the name was changed to Zanesville at a later date. Zane selected crossings of the Hocking and Scioto Rivers for his remaining sections.

Zanesville became the county seat of Muskingum County in 1804 and was incorporated in 1814. After Ohio gained statehood in 1803, Chillicothe was the state capital for several years. Zanesville was the capital from 1810 to 1812; then the capital was returned to Chillicothe.

Besides the noted author Zane Grey, the architect Cass Gilbert was also born in Zanesville. His birth date was November 24, 1859. Cass Gilbert was the architect of many important buildings in the eastern United States. A partial list includes: Woolworth Building, New York City; Central Public Library, St. Louis, Missouri; State Capitol, St. Paul, Minnesota; Public Library, Detroit, Michigan;

West Virginia State Capitol, Charleston, West Virginia; and many more. Cass Gilbert died May 17, 1934.

In 1814 a Y-Bridge was built across the Licking and Muskingum Rivers where they joined in Zanesville. This bridge was in use more than a decade before the National Road was built to Zanesville. Increased traffic made it necessary to replace it, and the present Y-Bridge is the fourth at this location.

During the decades of river and canal traffic in the nineteenth century, the Muskingum River was a highway of commerce. Boats carried passengers, mail, and freight with stops at towns along the river.

In the late years of the eighteenth century when settlers began to push west into the Northwest Territory, the Muskingum River flowed through a wilderness inhabited by Indians. Bison, more commonly called buffalo, at one time numbered in the millions, many of them on the prairies and plains between the Mississippi River and the Rocky Mountains. On a smaller scale they could be found east of the Mississippi, mostly south of the Great Lakes.

The following excerpts are from the "Report of the Geological Survey of Ohio — Volume IV, published in 1882."

> *There is ample evidence of the former existence and abundance of the Buffalo in Northern Ohio; it occurred in other parts of the State. Colonel John May met with it on the Muskingum in 1788, and Atwater says "we had once the bison and the elk in vast numbers all over Ohio."*

> **Extirpation of the Bison** — *The Buffalo was not driven to the westward by the encroachments of settlements; a few herds may have migrated, but it is more probable it was exterminated, rather than driven from the central States.*

In a communication to Mr. J. A. Allen, Mr. George Graham stated:

> *"From all that I know of the early settlement and history of the West, I am under the impression that the buffalo disappeared from Ohio, Illinois, Indiana, and Kentucky about the year 1800."*

We drove through the village of Hopewell as we approached the western boundary of Muskingum County, and soon came to the village of Gratiot, named for Brigadier General Charles Gratiot. The National Road across Ohio was built under the supervision of the Engineering Corps of the War Department.

As we continued toward the west, our route was across the southern edge of Licking County, founded on March 1, 1808. Newark, which became the county seat, was laid out in 1801; when the National Road was surveyed in 1825 the town was bypassed. This resulted in slow development, but the growth of the town was spurred by the completion of the Ohio and Erie Canal a few years later. The Licking River flows through the county, and both the river and the county were named for the salt licks that were natural to the area.

After we entered the county we went through Brownsville, with its Old Coach Inn, a building that dates from the 1820s, then through Linnville and came to Jacksontown. North of here about two miles, on the highway to Newark, is the Dawes Arboretum, covering more than 1,100 acres. We did not visit the Arboretum on this trip but spent some time there on a previous trip some years before.

Buckeye Lake, with more than 3,500 acres of water, is a short distance south of Hebron, the next town on our route. Only the northern fringe of the lake is in Licking County; much of it is in Fairfield County and the remainder is in Perry County. West of Hebron we soon came to Kirkersville, then went on to Etna, and, after a few miles, entered Franklin County.

The route we followed since leaving the mountainous highlands west of Cumberland, Maryland, was over the Allegheny Plateau. The highway slopes gradually downward in western Pennsylvania, crossing intervening higher ridges and drops to 650 feet above sea level at Wheeling, West Virginia. Rising from the Ohio River, the road traverses the hills of eastern Ohio. In the vicinity of western Licking County and eastern Franklin County, the Allegheny Plateau blends into the Central Plains. Extending west from this area, the land is level to rolling and the elevation varies only a few hundred feet on the route we expected to follow through western Ohio and across Indiana, Illinois, and Missouri.

Franklin County was established by an act of the Ohio legislature on April 30, 1803, and its name honors Benjamin Franklin. Prior to this date, Lucas Sullivant had laid out the village of Franklinton in 1797, west of the Scioto River. It was located near the point where the Olentangy River joins the Scioto. Franklinton was made the county seat of the new county in 1803.

When Ohio became the seventeenth state on March 1, 1803, Chillicothe was the state capital. One provision of the new state constitution was that the capital would not be moved until 1808. By that date the legislature was to select a permanent site, at or near the center of the state. The selection was not made by 1808 and Chillicothe remained the capital. In February, 1810, an act was passed authorizing a commission that was to recommend a permanent site for the capital. In the meantime the city of Zanesville became the temporary capital of Ohio from 1810 to 1812.

The commissioners had many sites from which they could choose the new state capital. Worthington, now part of the Columbus metropolitan area, made a strong attempt to be selected as the home of the capital. Several other towns wanted to be the capital of Ohio, and these included Delaware, Newark, and Zanesville.

Franklinton, the county seat, had grown considerably in the fifteen years since it was founded, and the townspeople felt that the seat of state government should be located there. The members of the commission carefully considered this site but ruled against it because there was danger that at times of high water, the river might overflow and flood this low-lying area.

The site that was finally chosen for the state capital was across the Scioto River from Franklinton. A group of men who owned land there offered it to the state legislature. They also offered to develop plans for a town and to contribute a sum of money that would help defray the cost of the necessary government buildings. Although the people of Franklinton had failed in their effort to have the capital on their side of the river, later they backed the plan to establish it east of the Scioto. While the state capital is not located at the geographical center of Ohio, it is not many miles south of that point.

The Ohio legislature passed a resolution on January 20, 1812, that officially determined Columbus as the name of the state capital. In June of that year, at the beginning of the War of 1812, the first lots were sold in the town. The war delayed construction of the government buildings and the general assembly was not able to meet in Columbus until December 2, 1816. Prior to this, the town had been incorporated as a borough on February 10, 1816. During the time the state capital was being developed, Franklinton continued as the county seat of Franklin County, but in 1824 the county seat was moved to Columbus. Nearly a half century after this, Franklinton officially became part of Columbus. This was in 1870.

On March 3, 1834, Columbus was incorporated as a city. During the previous year the National Road had been completed to the capital of Ohio. For several years this highway had a strong influence on the growth of the city and other towns on this east-west route.

As mentioned on a previous page, we came through the southern part of Licking County into Franklin County. The city of Reynoldsburg is situated just west of the Franklin-Licking County boundary and adjoins the eastern border of Columbus.

The village of Reynoldsburg was laid out by Abiather V. Taylor in 1831, the same year that James C. Reynolds came from Zanesville. The new town was named for Reynolds, who opened the first store soon after he arrived; in 1833 he became the first postmaster. Reynoldsburg was incorporated in 1839.

This city is called the "Birthplace of the Tomato" because it was here that the tomato was developed as a commercial crop. Alexander W. Livingston, born in 1822 at Reynoldsburg, was an experienced gardener by his mid-twenties. For many years after this, he experimented with the wild tomato whose fruit was small, tough, and extremely sour. Finally, in 1870, at the age of 48, he was able to produce a new variety of commercial tomato. This breakthrough made it possible to raise tomatoes on a large scale as a field crop. In more than a century since then, the raising and canning of tomatoes has become an important industry in Ohio.

51

After spending some time in Reynoldsburg, we proceeded into Columbus, where our daughter has lived and worked for many years. Our plans were to visit her and remain in Columbus for several days, then continue our trip toward the west.

Population records of the fifty states indicate a total of fifteen cities or towns with the name of Columbus. Possibly there are other small towns or hamlets with this name that are not listed in the published records. The capital of Ohio is, by far, the largest, with a census count of 632,945 in 1990. Ohio has a Columbus Grove and a Columbus Park, and one other state has a Columbus City and a Columbus Junction. Only one state has a Columbus County, but nine states have a county whose county seat is named Columbus. Among the natural features in the United States, there is a Columbus Salt Marsh.

The Ohio Buckeye tree is native to the central states, particularly Ohio, and to regions of the Mississippi Valley. On October 2, 1953, this tree was officially named the state tree of Ohio. People who live in Ohio, or who are from Ohio, are often called Buckeyes, and Ohio State athletic teams are generally known as the Bucks or Buckeyes.

The year 1992 signified that 500 years had passed since the first journey of Christopher Columbus across the Atlantic Ocean, that resulted in the discovery of America. Starting in April, 1992, the city of Columbus commemorated this event with a six-month long celebration called Ameriflora '92. Franklin Park, east of the center of the city, was the site of this quincentenary celebration.

On our way to Springfield where we would see our fourth Madonna of the Trail Monument, we drove through Madison County. The first cabin was built here in 1796, and during the next fourteen years enough pioneers settled in the area to establish a county. This was done on March 1, 1810, and its name honored James Madison, fourth president of the United States, serving his first term at the time the county was formed. London, the county seat, was mapped out in 1811. The first town we passed through was West Jefferson and a few more miles brought us to Lafayette. The latter was established by William Minter, a veteran of the War for Independence.

The experienced frontier fighter, George Rogers Clark, was born at Charlottesville, Virginia, November 19, 1752. In 1778 and 1779 he led Americans against the British in present-day Indiana and Illinois. Indian war parties, aided by the British, attacked settlements in Kentucky during the summer of 1780, and the decision was made to retaliate with military force. Clark, with an army of about 1,000 men from Kentucky, crossed the Ohio River where Cincinnati is now situated, and on August 2, 1780, started north. The army marched in the direction of the large Indian town of Piqua on the Mad River, a few miles west of the present city of Springfield, in Clark County.

George Rogers Clark had his army on the march early in the morning of August 8. As the first troops neared the town they were attacked by the Indians hiding in the tall weeds. In a battle that lasted about three hours, both sides lost a number of men. After the Indians withdrew from the area, orders were given to completely destroy the town and the crops in the nearby fields. This victory over the Indians was important in opening the Northwest Territory to settlement, but it was many years later that pioneers were free from danger.

Soon after we left Madison County we came to Brighton, then South Vienna, in Clark County. At the latter place, the residents of Harmony Township and of the town have sponsored a flagpole, mounted on a base that has this inscription:

DEDICATED
TO ALL VETERANS
PAST   PRESENT   FUTURE

On March 1, 1818, Clark County, named for George Rogers Clark, was formed from parts of Champaign, Greene, and Madison Counties. The county was first settled in the late 1790s near the Mad River, and in 1803, Springfield, the county seat, was planned by James Demint. The dates 1803 and 1818 are open to question, as some historical records show 1801 as the year Springfield was planned, and March 1, 1817, as the date Clark County was formed.

The National Road was pushed on toward the west from Columbus after 1833 and reached Springfield in 1838. Work continued and the road was completed to the western limits of this city the next year.

The Madonna of the Trail Monument in Ohio is situated at the western side of Springfield and was dedicated on July 4, 1928. It was the first of the twelve monuments to be dedicated.

The inscription on one side relates this information:

THE NATIONAL ROAD
COMPLETED BY THE
FEDERAL GOVERNMENT
TO THIS POINT IN 1839.
FROM THIS POINT WESTWARD
BUILT BY THE STATES THROUGH
WHICH IT PASSES

The other inscription has this message:

THREE MILES SOUTHWEST OF HERE
GENERAL GEORGE ROGERS CLARK
COMMANDING
KENTUCKY FRONTIERSMEN
VANQUISHED THE SHAWNEE
CONFEDERACY AUGUST 8, 1780
RESULTING IN OPENING THE
NORTHWEST TERRITORY

This military action was described here on a previous page.

Our route after we left the Madonna Monument took us to the town of Brandt, situated in the southeast corner of Miami County. Here an Ohio Historical Marker commemorates the National Road.

THE OLD NATIONAL ROAD
You are now traveling U.S. 40, the Old National Road, used in the westward expansion of our country. In 1837 notice was given that this

54

section of the road would be constructed. A toll house was located at the east edge of Brandt.

After taking a photograph of the marker, we moved on and soon turned to the south and entered Montgomery County.

This county was established May 1, 1803, and named in honor of General Richard Montgomery of the American army. Early in the War for Independence at attack was made against the British at Quebec, Canada, on December 31, 1775. The Americans were defeated with heavy casualties, and in this battle General Montgomery was killed. Soon after the formation of the county, Dayton was made the county seat. The town was named for Jonathan Dayton, a soldier in the Revolutionary War who became an officer in the Continental army. Later he was a member of a group that bought land in 1795 at the site of the present city of Dayton. In April, 1796, the first settlers arrived. The town grew during the next few years and was incorporated February 12, 1805.

Going on south we entered the Dayton suburbs, but before we went into the center of the city we visited the Wright Brothers Memorial. This commemorates the achievement of the brothers who made the first successful flight of a powered machine that was heavier than air. The memorial was dedicated on August 19, 1940.

Wilbur Wright was born April 16, 1867, on a small farm about twenty miles northwesterly from Richmond, Indiana. His parents had moved the family to Dayton prior to the time Orville Wright was born on August 19, 1871. The boys grew up in Dayton, and both attended high school there. Although more than four years apart in age, they always worked closely together.

In 1889, they published a neighborhood weekly newspaper with Wilbur as editor and Orville as publisher; prior to this they had built the printing press. In 1892 they decided to sell bicycles and formed a company that soon was successful. They realized that as sales of bicycles increased they should be able to repair them, so their next step was to move into a larger building and set up a repair shop. The mechanical ability and know-how of the brothers increased steadily during these years. In 1895 they expanded their bicycle business once more when they went into manufacturing. During the next few years they produced several hundred bicycles and sold models in a range of prices.

At about the time they began to sell and service bicycles, the Wright brothers became interested in aeronautics. They read all of the available scientific material that they could find and spent many hours observing birds, particularly the vultures, hawks, and gulls, species that soar by taking advantage of rising air currents. Experiments were made with kites that they designed and built; later they tested their principle of control by using a small glider. It was their income from the bicycle business that allowed them to pursue their work in aeronautics.

By 1899 they were convinced that they needed an area such as a beach where a glider could be airborne, then could sail an indefinite distance and land without damage, and without danger to the operator. Officials of the Weather Bureau stated that on the Outer Banks of North Carolina there was a long stretch of sand, and that prevailing wind conditions should be favorable for flying.

In the fall of 1900 they went to Kitty Hawk, North Carolina, and experimented with their newly designed glider. About four miles south of Kitty Hawk, several sand dunes known as the Kill Devil Hills gave them an opportunity to test the glider with one of the brothers on board. They made repeated flights and were able to glide as far as 400 feet before landing. The glider did not sustain serious damage when it came down on the sandy ground, and neither of the brothers was injured.

When the Wright brothers traveled in 1901 from Dayton to their camp near the Kill Devil Hills, they brought parts with which they could assemble a larger glider. With this improved glider they made several hundred flights during that season.

The next phase of their flight experiments was to build an aircraft that would utilize power furnished by an engine. This was accomplished between October, 1902, and December, 1903. On December 17, 1903, with Orville Wright at the controls, the first engine-powered airplane made a flight of 120 feet in twelve seconds. The Wright brothers made three more flights that day. The fourth flight, piloted by Wilbur, covered 852 feet in 59 seconds.

In the years after the historic flights of the Wright brothers on that day in December, 1903, they built improved airplanes capable of longer and faster flights.

Wilbur Wright died at Dayton on May 30, 1912, at the age of 45. By that time the aviation industry was well on the way, but it was his brother Orville who was fortunate enough to see aviation develop as it did during the next third of a century.

In the First World War airplanes were used for checking enemy positions, and there were air battles between planes armed with machine guns. In the twenty years after the war, larger, faster, and safer planes were built and air traffic increased. Air power was important in deciding the outcome of World War II, both in the European theater and in the Pacific theater of operations. In 1944, as the war was entering its final stages, American aviation history was made when the first jet aircraft was tested.

Orville Wright lived to the age of 76 years and died at Dayton on January 30, 1948.

The Old Courthouse Museum (Montgomery County Historical Society), located in the central part of the city, is an example of nineteenth century architecture that we wanted to see while in Dayton. Construction of this Greek Revival building was finished in 1850.

In 1913, two events occurred in Dayton that had long-term results for the city. On Tuesday, March 25 of that year, after five days of heavy rain, the Great Miami River reached flood stage and poured into the city. Many lives were lost and property damage was extremely heavy. Following this catastrophe, long-range plans for flood control were made in cooperation with the legislature of Ohio. Almost nine years after the 1913 flood, the project that would prevent future floods was completed. Also in 1913, Dayton became the first large city in the United States to use the city manager method of government.

Our route after we left Dayton was through New Lebanon, and in a few miles we entered Preble County. Formed March 1, 1808, this county was named for Edward Preble, a naval officer of the United States. In 1801, Tripoli declared war against the United

States. Preble commanded a naval attack against Tripoli in 1804, the year prior to the end of the war.

We continued through West Alexandria to Eaton, the county seat of Preble County. Eaton had its start in 1806 and was named for William Eaton, a general in the American army who distinguished himself in the war against Tripoli.

The wooded Fort St. Clair State Memorial is about a mile west of Eaton. On November 6, 1792, a battle was fought near Fort St. Clair when Kentucky militia riflemen were attacked by more than 200 Indians. The Americans beat back the attacking Indians and held the fort.

After our visit to the state memorial we headed northwest of Eaton and went through New Hope and New Westville. These were the last towns on our route across Ohio, and scarcely two miles beyond New Westville we drove into Indiana.

Chapter 6

Indiana

In 1679, the French explorer Robert Cavelier, Sieur de La Salle, entered northern Indiana when his small party crossed from the Great Lakes to the Mississippi River by using the portage near present-day South Bend. French fur traders had engaged in trade with Indians in Wisconsin beginning in 1667, and it is possible that there was similar trade in Indiana in the late 1660s. In 1720 the French built a fort on the Wabash River a few miles southwest of present Lafayette. Two years after this, Fort Miami was put up where Fort Wayne now stands. Fort Vincennes was built in 1731 followed soon by a trading post. After the settlement was well established it was named for Sieur de Vincennes, the French soldier who was the founder of the military post.

At the close of the French and Indian War in 1763, England gained control of the territory north and west of the Ohio River. Small detachments of British soldiers were placed at points along the Mississippi River, and a garrison was stationed at Vincennes. During the Revolutionary War a force of less than 200 frontier soldiers, under Lt. Col. George Rogers Clark, changed the course of history. By their exploits and bravery, this large territory, that later became five states, came under the control of the United States following the American Revolution.

This historic military campaign started when George Rogers Clark loaded his 150 men into small boats in western Pennsylvania and moved down the Ohio River in the spring of 1778. He camped on an island near the future city of Louisville, Kentucky, until late June. Numerous individuals and families came down the river with Clark's flotilla, or soon after the camp was set up, and his intention was to add a large number of volunteers to his force. The number added was a disappointment, as only 35 or 40 men joined the expedition. On June 24, 1778, he left the island and continued down the Ohio River for four days and nights, going ashore at an abandoned fort, now the site of Fort Massac State Park in Illinois. He led his men overland in the direction of Fort Kaskaskia, a British outpost on the Mississippi River. The expedition had no horses so the men carried all of their equipment and food on this grueling six-day march through the wilderness. On the night of the Fourth of July they entered the fort without being discovered, and the detachment of British soldiers surrendered without a show of resistance.

Clark acted quickly and sent one of his officers with about thirty men to capture the fort at Cahokia, situated approximately sixty miles north of Fort Kaskaskia. The surprise attack was successful and the small force of British defenders surrendered peacefully.

The Americans had secured the Illinois country without using military force, but to achieve the result that George Rogers Clark wanted, the British post at Vincennes must be taken. He was told that the commander of the Vincennes fort had gone to the British headquarters at Detroit, and that the Vincennes troops had accompanied him. An influential church official traveled to Vincennes at once, and through his influence the people of the town joined the American cause.

It would appear from Clark's success during the summer and early autumn of 1778, that the Americans had effectively gained control of the Indiana-Illinois country, but this was not the case. When Lieutenant Governor Henry Hamilton heard about the loss of Vincennes, he led an army of British soldiers and their Indian allies from Fort Detroit. They traveled across the end of Lake Erie and up the Maumee River, made the portage across to the Wabash River, then followed this south to Vincennes. The few American troops holding Vincennes had no choice when confronted by this army, and on December 17, 1778, surrendered to the British.

It was in January that Clark received word concerning the loss of Vincennes. At about the same time, he had authentic information that Hamilton had allowed part of his army to return home until spring. Clark soon made a decision to go to Vincennes and make a surprise attack on the fort. With winter weather conditions as they were, the British leader would consider that such an attack was impossible.

On February 5, 1779, Clark started from Fort Kaskaskia with 170 men. More than half of this small army were Virginians, and most of the rest were French volunteers. In eighteen days they traveled 170 to 180 miles across the flooded prairies and river valleys, sinking into the mud and wading for miles in water up to or above their knees. It rained during several of the days and their clothing was saturated most of the time. Clark later used the expression "incredible hardships" in describing the expedition.

As Clark had surmised in planning the attack, the British felt secure in their stronghold, but this feeling of security vanished when an American rifleman shot one of the fort's defenders through a porthole. This was soon after dark on February 23 and the firing continued during the night. The American riflemen were protected from cannon fire by hiding behind embankments, and picked off the defenders of the fort one by one as they tried to fire their artillery pieces.

The next morning Clark sent a note to Hamilton, demanding that he surrender but this demand was turned down. The rifle fire started again and Hamilton sent a letter under a flag of truce. In the letter he proposed an armistice but Clark replied that the garrison must surrender unconditionally. The siege continued; then the British commander agreed to meet with Clark. Before the day was over Hamilton signed surrender papers, and at 10:00 a.m. the next morning, February 25, 1779, the British troops marched out of the fort. George Rogers Clark led a party of Americans into the fort, raised the American flag, and took possession of Vincennes for the United States.

Lt. Col. George Rogers Clark was 26 years old at the time Vincennes was captured. Born November 19, 1752, he lived to the age of 65 and died near Louisville, Kentucky, on February 13, 1818.

Indiana Territory was formed May 7, 1800. The territorial government began July 4 of that year, with Vincennes as the capital and William Henry Harrison as the first governor. In his long career of public service, Harrison, born February 9, 1773, served as a major general during the War of 1812. A few years after this he served in Congress, both in the House of Representatives and in the Senate. In 1840 he was elected President of the United States and was inaugurated March 4, 1841. He was able to serve only 31 days and died of pneumonia April 4, 1841, at the age of 68.

Vincennes was the capital of the territory until May 1, 1813, when the capital was moved to Corydon, in Harrison County. From the time of its formation as a territory the population continued to increase, and by December 14, 1815, when the territorial legislature requested that Congress consider statehood for Indiana, the population was more than 63,000. December 11, 1816, was the date that Indiana entered the Union as the 19th state, and the first governor was Jonathan Jennings. The state capital was at Corydon, site of the territorial capital. Most of the population of the new state had settled in the southern counties, and an early map of the state had this notation: "All the central and northern portions of the state belonged to the Indians."

Late in 1816, about the time that Indiana entered the Union, a future president of the United States became a resident of the new state. Abraham Lincoln was born February 12, 1809, near Hodgenville, Kentucky. When he was seven years old, his father, Thomas Lincoln, moved his family from Kentucky to Indiana. Their new home was in present-day Spencer County, just north of the Ohio River; here Abraham Lincoln grew to manhood.

As we left Ohio we entered Wayne County and quickly drove into Richmond. The territorial legislature passed an act on November 27, 1810, that organized this county, with an effective date of February 1, 1811. Its name honors General Anthony Wayne whose outstanding deeds during the American Revolution, and whose victory over the Indians in 1794, earned for him the descriptive name, "Mad Anthony." After Wayne County was organized, Salisbury was made the county seat; but by an act of the legislature on December 21, 1816, the county seat was changed to Centerville. In that same year, 1816, the town of Richmond was laid out. After more than fifty years, the county seat was moved from Centerville to Richmond, on August 15, 1873.

The fifth Madonna of the Trail Monument is located at the entrance to Glen Miller Park in Richmond. The dedication ceremony here took place on October 28, 1928.

The inscription on one panel reads:

THE FIRST TOLL-GATE
IN INDIANA
STOOD NEAR THIS SITE
ON THE NATIONAL ROAD

This is the statement on the other panel:

A NATION'S HIGHWAY!
ONCE A WILDERNESS TRAIL
OVER WHICH HARDY PIONEERS
MADE THEIR PERILOUS WAY
SEEKING NEW HOMES
IN THE DENSE FORESTS
OF THE GREAT NORTHWEST

The highest point in the state of Indiana, at 1,257 feet, is situated in Wayne County approximately twelve miles north of Richmond. The total difference of elevation in Indiana is 937 feet, and the lowest point is 320 feet. This is the Ohio River in the southwest corner of the state.

We left Richmond and soon came to Centerville, mentioned a few paragraphs back. Mapped out in 1814, this town received its name because it is situated close to the center of Wayne County. Proceeding, we drove through Pennville, then entered East Germantown. In 1918, this town was given the name Pershing, in honor of John Pershing, commanding general of American forces in Europe during World War I. This name did not remain permanent, and current highways maps show this as East Germantown.

After East Germantown we came to Cambridge City, established in 1836 as a station on the Whitewater Canal, then to nearby Mt. Auburn laid out in 1864. Dublin, where the first settlers arrived in 1821, was our last town in Wayne County, and we soon entered Henry County.

The first settlers arrived in this area in 1818, and Henry County originated on December 31, 1821. Its name honors Patrick Henry of "Give me liberty or give me death" fame. New Castle has been the county seat since the county was formed. As mentioned previously, Wilbur Wright was born northwest of Richmond and his birthplace is in Henry County.

Straughn was our first town in this county. It was laid out in 1868 and was named Straughn's Station. Merriman Straughn was an early settler here. Lewisville, a few miles west, received its name from the first name of the man who started the town, Lewis Freeman.

We drove to Dunreith, which was called Coffin's Station after the settlement had its start in 1865. It was named for Emery Dunreith Coffin and his middle name ended up as the name of the town. Ogden and South Raysville were the next villages as we continued west, and in a few minutes we were in Knightstown.

Charles Austin Beard, the author of many historical works, was born at Knightstown, November 27, 1874. In the early 1890s, Beard and his older brother were in charge of publishing a newspaper in Knightstown. Following this, during the next twenty years, Charles A. Beard spent several years in England. Back in the United States, he attended Columbia University where he received degrees and later became a professor. In those years he wrote a number of books on politics and European history.

The last 25 years of his life were largely devoted to traveling and to writing additional books. He also wrote articles for several well-known magazines. Beard wrote on a wide range of subjects and was very knowledgeable concerning the Constitution of the United States and the Civil War. Charles Austin Beard died at New Haven, Connecticut, September 1, 1948.

Hancock, the next county to the west, was established by a legislative act on January 26, 1827. Its name honors John Hancock whose signature was so boldly written on the Declaration of Independence. Soon after we entered this county we came to the village of Charlottesville, founded in 1830, and then Cleveland, another small village. The former is the namesake of the city of Charlottesville, Virginia, and the latter was known as Portland for about twenty years, until the name became Cleveland, during the 1850s.

We reached the city of Greenfield soon after we left Cleveland. Greenfield was made the county seat of Hancock County on April 11, 1828, by the action of a committee that chose the seat of government for the county.

James Whitcomb Riley, "The Hoosier Poet," was born October 7, 1849, at Greenfield. His father, Reuben Riley, had come as a pioneer to the village in 1844, bringing his bride, and it was here that Reuben started his law practice.

James Whitcomb Riley was not destined to become a strong, muscular individual, and his father was disappointed as the lad grew up because he could not handle the rough jobs that would develop him physically. Years later, Reuben, the lawyer, got over his early disappointment after his son became a successful poet.

The boy attended school in Greenfield but was not considered by his teachers as an outstanding scholar. Applying himself to the daily school routine was difficult for this young student who had a taste for interesting reading and a distaste for textbooks. In the vernacular of a later day, it could be said that he marched to the beat of a different drummer. The Riley homelife was conducive to reading, with good books available, and he read many of them. While he was still quite young he discovered that the local newspaper office was an interesting and educational place to visit.

After he finished his regular schooling there was an interval of several years when he tried to determine the course that his life would follow. Most young men of his age tried to find their place in the business world, or in farming or industry, but the routine involved in such lines of endeavor did not appeal to him. He had writing ability and a special capacity for composing rhymes, but it is doubtful that he even considered that he could make a living that way.

He took several trips in his home state of Indiana, and some were of several months duration. Along with his ability to write, this talented young man could paint and draw. On one of these trips he painted signs and advertisements for a traveling doctor.

65

Another tour was with a partner in the sign-painting business, and once he joined a troupe of strolling actors.

James Whitcomb Riley matured during these years and sharpened his powers of observation, and it is certain that he met many types of human beings. In later years he would be able to draw on his memory for numerous mental pictures of people that he could introduce to the public through his poems.

It was in the course of the years of traveling that his natural inclination to write gradually took over. After several years he visited a few newspaper offices in the larger towns and became well acquainted with the editors. Many of his earliest poetic works were published by these editors.

A real break on his way to success came when his poems began to appear in a leading Indianapolis newspaper. Some were written in dialect and in others his technique was to use poetically correct language.

His poems became a popular feature of the newspaper and before he was thirty years old he moved from Greenfield to Indianapolis. The newspaper office became his headquarters until his middle fifties and many of his poems were written there. Some of his most popular poems were written in dialect about his childhood years while growing up in the Riley family. During his lifetime he wrote more than one thousand poems, and, over the years, collections of his poems were published and sold in large numbers.

After his success as a poet was established he was in demand as a speaker. For several years he appeared before audiences, not only in Indiana, but in Boston and New York and other cities. Large crowds came to hear him but it was a tiring life. He gave up the professional lecture tour and returned to Indianapolis prior to 1910 so he could live more quietly and would not have to travel.

James Whitcomb Riley died at his home in Indianapolis, July 22, 1916.

More than three quarters of a century after his death, this Indiana poet is remembered by the people of his home state. On Main Street in Greenfield, in front of the home where the poet was born, a plaque commemorates his life:

Birthplace
JAMES WHITCOMB RILEY
"The Hoosier Poet"
October 7, 1849 — July 22, 1916
Editor, author, poet, lecturer and entertainer. One of the best known Hoosiers of all time. Riley first wrote under the name of "Benj. F. Johnson of Boone" and was famous for his use of Hoosier dialect.

In early October of each year the Riley Festival is scheduled in Greenfield to celebrate the birthday of this poet, born nearly 150 years ago.

Going on toward Indianapolis from Greenfield, we drove through the village of Gem and soon left Hancock County and entered Marion County. The legislative act that set up this county was passed December 31, 1821. Its name honors General Francis Marion whose guerrilla tactics in North and South Carolina during the Revolutionary War helped assure victory for the American cause. The population of this county exceeds that of any other county in the state. The large city of Indianapolis, the state capital as well as the county seat, accounts for much of this population. We were in Cumberland, with a population of about 5,000 just after we crossed the county boundary. Laid out in 1831 on the National Road or Cumberland Road, the town received the latter name.

When Indiana became the 19th state on December 11, 1816, the territorial capital was at Corydon, near the Ohio River. This became the state capital of Indiana, and, in 1820, the legislature made a decision to pick a site for the future capital of the state. The United States Congress had given the new state four sections of land on which a new captial could be built. The four sections could be chosen from any public land of the United States that had not previously been sold. On January 11, 1820, a commission of ten men was appointed by the legislature to find the proper place for the permanent seat of government. One commissioner was selected from each of the following ten counties: Clark, Dearborn, Fayette, Gibson, Harrison, Jackson, Knox, Posey, Switzerland, and Wayne.

On Wednesday, May 17, 1820, one of the commissioners left Corydon on horseback, accompanied by the governor of Indiana, Jonathan Jennings. The two men traveled northward, made an overnight stop, and the next day met two other commissioners at Vallonia, in Jackson County. The party continued north over the weekend, and on Monday, May 22, arrived at their designated meeting place on the White River several miles north of present-day Indianapolis. Here they met the other commissioners and prepared to carry on their work.

The members of the commission spent several days in the White River-Falls Creek (at that time called Fall Creek) area, and they were particularly interested in the land that surrounded the junction of the two streams. On Saturday, May 27, they made their decision concerning the site for the capital. At their meeting the next day they learned that it would be ten days before the surveyors could finish their work. The commissioners then adjourned for more than a week.

At their meeting on June 7, 1820, the members of the commission signed the report that would be submitted to the legislature. The site they had selected was on a navigable stream and was quite near the geographic center of Indiana.

After studying the report turned in by the commission, the legislature voted to approve it and then proceeded to the next step. This was to select a name for the new capital. Many names were put in the hopper, and after much debate and argument, "Indianapolis" was chosen.

The commissioners had chosen wisely, and this would be proven after the passage of time, but the location they had selected was in the wilderness. There were only a few scattered cabins, and forests surrounded the site for miles in every direction. The nearest settlements were about sixty miles away. An artist's concept, "Indianapolis, the Capital in the Woods," depicted a lone log cabin surrounded by trees that were covered with snow.

From December 14, 1815, the date when the territorial legislature made its move toward statehood, to 1820, the population of Indiana had more than doubled. In the latter year there were over 147,000 inhabitants. Except for a few settlements along the Wabash and White Rivers, most of this population lived within fifty miles of the Ohio River.

Settlers found that the soil was suitable for farming, but clearing the land was extremely difficult. There were few roads, and at times these were almost impassable. Organized resistance by Indian tribes east of the Mississippi River had about ended but massacres by bands of Indians still occurred. If isolated settlers were spared, many times their horses and cattle were stolen, leaving them with no way to cultivate the land.

In April, 1821, less than a year after the commission finished its task, surveyors began to lay out the city-to-be. Streets were mapped out through the trees and lots were measured off. Prior to this, after the location of the capital had been determined in 1820, the news had traveled to settlements in the state, and to the east and south beyond the state's boundaries. Settlers arrived, many of them prospective buyers of the lots that would be sold. The sale of these lots began on October 8, 1821; by early 1822 the population of the town was about 500 inhabitants.

On December 31, 1821, the legislature established Marion County and made Indianapolis the county seat. There was a dire need for roads, and the legislature appropriated funds to build the roads that would connect Indianapolis with the outside world. The town was beginning to grow. Soon the county seat had a store, a tavern, and a post office. A lawyer had opened his office, and the town's first newspaper had appeared in January, 1822. Although there were no free schools supported by public taxation, some of the citizens made arrangements to open a school and keep it operating. Church services were started soon after the first settlers arrived, and by 1823 three churches had been organized.

When the legislature met at Corydon in January, 1824, an order was issued to move the state capital to Indianapolis by January 10, 1825. In late October or early November the state's documents and records were loaded in wagons at the State House in Corydon. The trip to the new capital took eleven days over nearly impassable roads, but before December first the state government was set up and ready for business in the Marion County Courthouse, and the legislature met there early in 1825.

By that time progress was being made in getting the town ready to be the seat of government, but much needed to be done. Only one or two streets had been cleared, and even there some stumps of trees had not been removed. There was mud everywhere after rains or after snow had melted.

By the time the state government had been moved to Indianapolis there were two or three taverns in the town. These were popular meeting places during the long winter evenings. Before the first session of the legislature had adjourned, one of the taverns burned down. This served as a reminder that the community was in danger of being destroyed if a serious fire should start. The town had no money to buy fire fighting equipment so a bucket brigade was organized. It was ten years later that the town purchased its first fire engine.

At the time the new capital was surveyed and lots were sold, it showed signs of fairly rapid growth, but this pattern was not maintained. As mentioned previously, the population was approximately 500 early in 1822. Growth of the new town was slow, and in February, 1826, the count was less than 800 people. There was an increase of population in Indianapolis during the 1830s when the National Road was built through the state. It was in the decade of the 1840s that the railroad reached the capital city. Industrial activity increased, resulting in population growth.

During the seven-year interval from 1818 to 1825 that construction of the National Road was stalled at the Ohio River, the state of Indiana had moved its seat of government from Corydon to Indianapolis. When Congress passed the act on March 3, 1825, to finance the road to Zanesville, Ohio, and also to extend the survey to the capital of Missouri, it indicated that federal funds would be made available to continue the project. The act ordered that the road must pass the seats of government of Ohio, Indiana, and Illinois. This made it certain that Columbus, Ohio; Indianapolis, Indiana; and Vandalia, Illinois would be on the route of the new road.

When the route of the National Road was made certain by the survey, businesses were started and towns were laid out on or near the road. This undoubtedly is the reason that many towns along the

National Road in Indiana have a history dating from the late 1820s to about 1838.

In every year from 1829 to 1838, Congress set aside money for the National Road in Indiana. The Act of May 31, 1830, appropriated funds for opening and grading the road in Indiana, "Commencing at Indianapolis, and progressing with the work to the eastern and western boundaries of the State."

As provided in this Act of Congress, Indianapolis, the capital established in the wilderness only a few years before, was the center from which the National Road was built to the east and to the west, over a period of nearly a decade.

The legislature held its meetings in the Marion County Courthouse for several years. In 1832 work was started on a capitol building, and the legislature was able to hold its meetings in this new capitol in 1835. The town was incorporated in 1836 under a special charter granted by the legislature. The financial panic of the following year hit Indianapolis very hard and business was in the doldrums until 1843.

After 27 years, the capital reached an estimated population of 6,000 by February, 1847. At that time the legislature allowed the voters of Indianapolis to decide whether to adopt a city charter. The vote was in favor of the charter that set up a municipal government with a council headed by the mayor. One of the first moves of the new city government was to improve the streets. In the years that had elapsed since the founding of the capital, very little had been done to turn the streets into thoroughfares. There were stumps even yet in some of the principal streets, and there was mud or dust, depending on the amount of rainfall or lack of it. Plans were carried out to remove the stumps, and the streets in the center of the city were graded. Many wagonloads of gravel made these central streets passable even in wet weather, and sidewalks were made alongside these streets. Besides the program of street improvements the city government made the first moves that resulted later in a system of free public schools in the capital.

The population of Indiana in 1850 was more than 988,000, and by 1860 had increased to over 1,350,000. During the Civil

War the state furnished thousands of men for the Union army and sustained many casualties.

The raid of Confederate General John Morgan into Ohio that resulted in his capture, followed his invasion of Indiana, as we noted. Soon after Morgan and his forces reached the Ohio River at Brandenburg, Kentucky, on July 7, 1863, he was able to capture two Ohio River steamers. By the evening of July 8 his men, with their horses, had crossed the river and were encamped a few miles south of Corydon.

The next morning, Thursday, July 9, in a battle near Corydon, the Confederate forces heavily outnumbered the local defenders. There were casualties on both sides and the Indiana militia surrendered more than 300 men. Morgan's cavalry took over the town, looted stores, and rounded up more than 500 horses in the surrounding countryside. Spreading his forces, Morgan moved north through the adjacent counties, plundering houses and farms and capturing more horses. On July 10 his cavalry entered Salem, in Washington County, and here the destruction was even worse than at Corydon. Railroad tracks were torn up, bridges were destroyed, businesses were robbed, and part of the town was destroyed by fire.

Swinging northeast, the invaders reached Vernon, in Jennings County, on July 11 but this town was well defended. Morgan turned east and entered Versailles, in Ripley County, on Sunday, July 12, then left the town that afternoon. During the afternoon of Monday, July 13, 1863, Morgan's cavalry entered Ohio at Harrison in Hamilton County and soon pushed on to the east.

During the 1850s and 1860s, Indianapolis grew at a rapid pace, and in 1870 the population was more than 48,000. By the turn of the twentieth century it had grown to nearly 171,000.

The State House that was completed in 1835 was outgrown in four decades. In 1877 the General Assembly voted to replace it and in 1885 the present State House was completed. Many business blocks, private residences, and public buildings were built. By the end of the nineteenth century, the city had developed into a large commercial and governmental center of this midwestern state. While the State House was in the last stage of construction, the

General Assembly passed an act in 1887 that authorized the building of the Soldiers and Sailors Monument, situated near the center of downtown, not far from the Capitol. This landmark was designed by the architect Bruno Schmidt, and was dedicated May 15, 1902, with thousands of Indiana citizens in attendance.

In the early years of the present century the automobile became very important as a means of transportation in the United States. Automobile factories started production in Indianapolis, as in many other industrial centers of the country, but within a few years, the city could not compete successfully in this mass production industry.

In 1909, the Motor Speedway was built in Indianapolis, for testing and racing automobiles. This has been a success for many decades. The annual 500 mile race held there draws many thousands of racing enthusiasts to the city. In the long history of this event, the race has been a testing ground for various automotive improvements.

The first of these races was held in 1911, when the winning speed for the distance was 74.602 miles per hour. In 1912 it was 78.719 per hour and in 1913, 75.933 per hour. Since 1914 the average speed of the winner has never been less than 82.474 miles per hour, the winning speed of that year. There has been a general increase in speed ever since 1911, but this has not occurred every year. At times, the speed attained in a given year has been the highwater mark for the next several races. The record speed for the Indianapolis 500, through the year 1998, is 185.981 miles per hour, attained in 1990. During World War I the race was not held in 1917 or 1918, and in the World War II years, no race was held in 1942 through 1945.

The population growth of Indianapolis and its development as a progressive city have continued throughout the twentieth century, and the 1990 census count was 731,327.

Hendricks County, entered after we left Indianapolis, was founded by the legislature December 20, 1823, two years after Marion County had its start. It was named for William Hendricks, the first representative to Congress from Indiana after statehood. He served in the House of Representatives from December 11, 1816,

73

to July 25, 1822; was governor of Indiana, 1822 to 1825; and was in the U.S. Senate, 1825 to 1827. Danville has been the county seat of Hendricks County since the county was established.

The city of Plainfield was planned in 1839 and became a stagestop on the National Road after this road was built across the state. After we left Plainfield we continued west to Belleville, started in 1829, then to Stilesville, in the southwestern corner of Hendricks County. The latter town was named for Jeremiah Stiles.

We soon were in Putnam County, formed December 31, 1821, on the day that Marion County was established by the legislature. In April of the next year Greencastle was made the county seat. The name of this county honors Major General Israel Putnam of the Continental Army. Born in Salem, Massachusetts, on January 7, 1718, Putnam was commissioned as an officer in the Connecticut militia, and later served in the French and Indian War. During the Battle of Bunker Hill on June 17, 1775, General Putnam was active in planning the American defense against repeated charges by the British troops. General Israel Putnam died May 29, 1790, at Brooklyn, Connecticut.

Mount Meridian dates from 1833. This was the first town on our route through Putnam County. It was named Carthage when it was mapped out. Two years later when the post office was installed, the name was changed in order to avoid confusion with another Carthage already established in Indiana. We went through Putnamville, Manhattan, and Reelsville as we continued through Putnam County. These towns were all started after the National Road was constructed west of Indianapolis.

As we approached the Putnam-Clay County boundary we stopped at a plaque that was placed there by the Indiana Sesquicentennial Commission in 1966:

10 O'CLOCK
TREATY LINE
Runs northwest-southeast through this point. On September 30, 1809, Indiana Territorial Governor, William Henry Harrison, obtained for the United States almost three million acres from the Potawatomi, Delaware and Miami tribes.

74

Harmony was our first town in Clay County. Then we drove through Knightsville, planned in 1867 by A. W. Knight. Clay County was named for Henry Clay, the statesman from Kentucky, and was established February 12, 1825. Several weeks after this when the county organization was completed, Bowling Green was made the county seat. More than fifty years later, Brazil became the seat of county government on January 26, 1877. Our route through the city took us past the Clay County Courthouse.

Several miles west of Brazil, we entered Vigo County and soon came to Seelyville. Plans for this town were drawn up by Jonas Seely in 1871, four years after the post office was opened with Seely as the first postmaster. The name of this county honors Francis Vigo, born in Italy December 3, 1747. Vigo was a successful fur trader who aided the Americans by furnishing money and supplies during the Revolutionary War. At the time of George Rogers Clark's campaign that resulted in the capture of Vincennes, Indiana, Francis Vigo was able to furnish information to Clark that helped assure the success of the mission. Francis Vigo died at Vincennes, March 22, 1836.

About 1720, the French selected a plateau on the east bank of the Wabash River as the location of a settlement. They named it Terre Haute, "high land." In September, 1811, a site for a fort was selected by General William Henry Harrison, north of the present city of Terre Haute. By 1816 a number of settlers had arrived in the area, and later that year the town of Terre Haute was mapped out. Vigo County was set up January 21, 1818, by an act of the legislature; two months later Terre Haute became the county seat.

We were near the Indiana State University campus as we drove through Terre Haute, and soon crossed the Wabash River into West Terre Haute. This town was laid out in 1836. The original name was Macksville, derived from Samuel McQuilkin, the man who started the town. Later the name was chosen that describes the location of the town. After we left West Terre Haute we were soon in Illinois.

Chapter 7

Illinois

The French explorers and traders of the seventeenth century were the first Europeans to see Illinois. Possibly some fur trading was carried on with the Indians about 1670, but it was Louis Joliet and Jacques Marquette who left a record of their travels. On June 17, 1673, they reached the Mississippi River at the mouth of the Wisconsin River after going across Wisconsin. The small party of explorers floated down the Mississippi, and it is believed that they went beyond the point where the Ohio River joins the Mississippi.

On July 17, a month after they started their journey downstream, they began the slow trip north, rowing against the current of the Mississippi River. When they arrived at the mouth of the Illinois River, they followed this river north, then northeast. After passing through the area of present-day Chicago and proceeding north on Lake Michigan, they returned to Green Bay in September.

As was related here in the Indiana segment, the French built forts and established settlements in that future state during the 1720s and 1730s. In those two decades, forts and settlements were set up by the French in Illinois. Most of this activity took place near the Mississippi River.

The most important fortification, Fort de Chartres, was built in 1720, near the east bank of the Mississippi River. This was in the vicinity of Prairie du Rocher, about fifty miles south of St. Louis, Missouri. Most of the French population of Illinois lived between the village of Cahokia and the larger town of Kaskaskia, about sixty miles south of Cahokia. Cahokia was about a mile east of the Mississippi River, across the river from St. Louis.

The French population, at peace with the Indians of that area, lived a simple life and had few luxuries, but enjoyed a measure of prosperity for many years. Good crops were raised in the fertile farmland, and New Orleans was a ready market for supplies shipped down the river from Illinois.

The French and Indian War, 1756 to 1763, was mostly decided on the battlefields of the east and in Canada, but after the treaty was signed, control of the Illinois country passed to the British. There was a delay of more than two years after February 10, 1763, the date of the treaty, before the English authorities were able to assert their rule over this western territory. In October, 1765, a company of British troops arrived at Fort de Chartres on the Mississippi River, and the garrison of about twenty French soldiers surrendered.

When a spring flood damaged Fort de Chartres, the British soldiers stationed there were moved to Kaskaskia. Here they built a stockade that served as a fortification. Cahokia, across the river from St. Louis, was only lightly defended by the British. On the Wabash River, Vincennes was well fortified by the British army.

The military campaigns led by George Rogers Clark in 1778-1779 during the Revolutionary War, were described here in preceding pages. With the signing of the treaty on September 3, 1783, ending the War for Independence, the United States was recognized as an independent nation, with the Mississippi River as the western boundary of the country.

The population of Illinois increased slowly during the last years of the eighteenth century and first years of the next century. On February 3, 1809, Congress passed an act that created the Territory of Illinois with Kaskaskia as the capital, and Ninian Edwards became the Territorial Governor on April 24, 1809. The population of Illinois was under 10,000 in 1809 when the territory was established, but increased steadily during the next few years, and a request was made to Congress to allow the formation of a state government. The requirement of 60,000 inhabitants for admission as a state was changed to 40,000 by an act passed early in 1818. On December 3, 1818, Illinois became the 21st state, with Kaskaskia the capital.

In the first state election, held in September, 1818, several weeks prior to statehood, Shadrach Bond was elected as the first governor of Illinois and Pierre Menard as the lieutenant governor. On

October 5, 1818, the first general assembly of the new state met at Kaskaskia.

Clark County, named for George Rogers Clark, was our first county in Illinois. This county was established March 22, 1819, and Marshall has been its county seat since 1837. The three states on our route since we crossed the Ohio River were the first that were formed from the Northwest Territory. Each of these, Ohio, Indiana, and Illinois, has honored George Rogers Clark by naming a county for him.

About ten miles after we entered Illinois we came to Marshall, laid out in 1835, and named for John Marshall. For 34 years, from 1801 to 1835, John Marshall served on the Supreme Court of the United States. This county seat is at the junction of two highways important in the history of Illinois. In the days of the stagecoach, present-day State Route No. 1 was the route from Chicago to Vincennes, south of Marshall. The National Road, later designated as U.S. 40, carried eastbound and westbound traffic through the town. Both of these highways are still well-traveled, but their early importance has diminished.

We continued to the west through the village of Clark Center, then in a few miles reached Martinsville, planned by Joseph Martin in 1833. This town became a stage stop after the National Road was built through the area. The last town in Clark County, as we moved on toward the west, was Casey. Incorporated in 1871, the town was named for Zadok Casey, a former lieutenant governor of Illinois.

We crossed the boundary between Clark and Cumberland counties soon after we left Casey. Cumberland County was formed March 2, 1843, and named for the Cumberland or National Road. About ten miles beyond Casey, we came to Greenup. William C. Greenup was secretary of the Senate in the first general assembly of the state. During the 1830s he supervised construction of the Cumberland Road across Illinois to Vandalia. In 1835 Greenup and his business partner mapped out this town that bears his name, and offered lots to the public. For the first twelve years after Cumberland County was established, Greenup was the county seat, but from 1855 to the present time, Toledo has been the seat of county government. After passing through Greenup the highway soon crosses the Embarras River and proceeds to the village of Jewett.

It was at some point a few miles west of Jewett that we passed a man and woman carrying packs. I have done some hiking and cross-country walking, so I pulled ahead of them and stopped in order to speak to them. "I'm curious. Are you hiking a long distance?" They said, "Yes. We expect to hike to Kansas." They also mentioned that each year they planned a hiking trip. I enjoyed our brief conversation, and they were glad that I stopped. If they ever read this they may remember the driver of the car from Arizona who talked to them in Illinois.

About seven miles beyond Jewett the road enters the northeast corner of Effingham County and soon passes through the small village of Montrose. After several miles it reaches Teutopolis, a town settled in 1839 by a number of Germans who came from Cincinnati, Ohio, along with others who migrated from Germany. In 1860, a theological school, Saint Joseph Seminary, was founded here, located a short distance from this highway.

Effingham, the city we now entered, is the county seat of Effingham County. Both the city and the county have the name of an English peer of Revolutionary War days, the Earl of Effingham. This member of the British nobility was a supporter of the Americans in the War for Independence. The county was established February 15, 1831, and the state legislature made Ewington the county seat. In 1852 when the railroad was constructed, the tracks were laid to the east and bypassed Ewington. A village was laid out on the railroad and two years later it was incorporated and given the same name as the county. In 1860, Effingham was made the county seat, and the county records were moved from Ewington.

We were acquainted with Effingham, having stayed there overnight on one of our previous trips through Illinois. Soon we drove out of the city and went across the Little Wabash River. The town of Dexter, a few miles west of Effingham, is shown on an early road map of this area, and also appears on an up-to-date map that we were carrying. On another modern map, the town of Keptown is shown instead of Dexter. We came to Keptown, and, after driving a distance on a nearby side road, we went past the Dexter Methodist Church.

Continuing westward, we soon came to Altamont, established in 1872 and named for a hillock about a mile from the townsite. Leaving Effingham County, we entered Fayette County, another of the counties in the United States named in honor of the Marquis de Lafayette. This county was formed February 14, 1821. Our first town here was St. Elmo, started in 1830 by settlers from Kentucky. Brownstown, several miles beyond St. Elmo, was our next town. We soon came to Bluff City as we approached Vandailia, the county seat.

At the time Illinois became the 21st state with Kaskaskia as the capital, the population had been increasing steadily. Many people were settling farther north, and during the first general assembly it was decided that the capital should be moved to a point that would be nearer the center of population. The federal government at Washington approved a grant of land for laying out a town that would continue as the capital for the next twenty years. A commission of five members in the spring of 1819 chose a site on the west bank of the Kaskaskia River, more than eighty miles northeast of Kaskaskia. Surveyors soon laid out lots for the new town in this forested area, and a two-story frame capitol building was put up. The state records were hauled from Kaskaskia on a wagon. In some places it was necessary to cut down trees to open a road through the forest. In December, 1820, the general assembly met at this new capital in the town of Vandalia.

During the decade after Vandailia was made the state capital the population of Illinois increased rapidly. From a population of 55,162 in 1820, the state had grown to more than 157,000 by 1830. Many new counties were created and the northern part of Illinois was becoming populated.

The capitol building, put up in 1820 in Vandalia, burned down in December, 1823. In the next summer a new building was hurriedly constructed. Ten years later this building became unsafe, and in the summer of 1836 construction began on a third statehouse, larger and better constructed than its predecessors. This building has stood the test of time, and more than a century and a half later is still standing.

81

Early in 1830, Abraham Lincoln arrived in Macon County, Illinois, a county that was established January 19, 1829. The county seat is the city of Decatur. His father had decided to leave Indiana, and Abraham drove the oxen that were hitched to a wagon, loaded with the meager possessions of three related families.

It had been a difficult journey of fifteen days, some of it through deep mud, and there were several stream crossings. Thomas Lincoln, the father, with the help of Abraham and the other family members, built a new house on a small farm about ten miles west of Decatur.

Abraham was now past 21 years old. He had certainly done his duty by his father and now he wanted to live his own life. He did not move far away but worked at various jobs in the area where he lived. The following winter he was employed to split rails, and walked several miles each day in going to his work and returning home.

In February, 1831, less than a year after he arrived in Illinois, Lincoln was offered an opportunity to go to New Orleans. He and two friends were to take a loaded flatboat down the Mississippi River. This would be his second trip to New Orleans. In the spring of 1828, while he was still in Indiana, he had been hired as a boat hand on a similar trip down the Mississippi River.

The boat that they were to take to New Orleans had not been built as was planned, so the three young men built a boat during the next month. About the middle of April, with the owner on board with them, they started in a westerly direction down the Sangamon River to the Illinois River. Going south past Beardstown, they reached the Mississippi at a point northwest of St. Louis, then floated down this great river. A few stops were made on the way down the Mississippi, among them Memphis, Vicksburg, and Natchez. They arrived at New Orleans with their cargo in May, 1831, and in the month of June they boarded a steamboat for the trip north.

Several weeks after his return from the boat trip down the river, he was in the small town of New Salem in Menard County, about twenty miles northwest of Springfield, Illinois. It was election day and he was spending some time near the voting place, and happened to be at the right place at the right time. The election officials needed a clerk. After they talked to him, he was appointed to that position. It was here that he performed the first official public act of his many years of public service.

Abraham Lincoln announced in March, 1832, that he would be a candidate for the legislature at Vandalia, as a member from Sangamon County. Later, during the spring and early summer of that year, Lincoln served as a volunteer in the Illinois militia in the Black Hawk War, part of the time as a Captain. After his return home, this service during the war kept his name before the public. He was also gaining a reputation as a public speaker. He knew that he was not well-known in parts of the voting district, and he was urged to make a canvass of the county in order to meet more of the voters. At a public sale in a small town west of Springfield, this 23-year-old candidate made a brief speech that outlined his political principles.

He opened the speech to his fellow citizens by referring to himself as being humble, and said that many of his friends had wanted him to try for election to the Legislature. Lincoln said that it would not take long to explain his politics, and that he was in favor of a national bank. Also he believed in the internal-improvement system and favored a high protective tariff. He stated that these were his sentiments, the political principles he believed in, and that, if he was elected, he would be thankful to the voters. After a few more words, the speech ended.

The announcement of Abraham Lincoln's candidacy in March that year had been in the form of a printed circular addressed to the people of Sangamon County. In this document he said that having become a candidate to be their Representative in the next General Assembly of the state, it was his duty to make known his sentiments concerning local affairs.

Lincoln told them there were two subjects in particular on which he wanted to express his feelings. One of these was the improvement of navigation on the Sangamon River, and the other subject was that of education for all. Of these, he said it was his view that education was the most important subject that the people could consider. People should have sufficient education to enable them to read the histories of this country and of other countries of the world, so they would be able to judge the value of our free institutions. This would also enable them to read the Scriptures, as well as other works.

In this published statement, he said that it was his desire that morality and enterprise would become more general by means of education. He would be gratified if he could contribute something that would bring these results sooner.

The published paper concerning his candidacy concluded by saying that his ambition was to be esteemed by his fellowmen, by making himself worthy of their esteem. He was young and not well-known, and if the people should choose not to elect him, he knew how to accept disappointment, without having his pride hurt too much. The printed announcement was signed, A. LINCOLN.

Abraham Lincoln was defeated in his bid for the seat in the legislature that year. In his own neighborhood he was well supported and received almost the entire vote, but in the rest of the district where he was not well-known, he was roundly defeated. This came as no surprise to him. As a young politician, the experience he had gained was worthwhile. He was especially pleased with the vote in his home district, and now was better known than before in other parts of the county.

No attempt will be made here to give a detailed account of Lincoln's activities after his defeat in the 1832 election. He went into the grocery business with a partner, the store was a failure, his partner left town, and Lincoln had to assume the debt of the failed business. He studied and trained to become a surveyor, and soon was appointed as assistant to the surveyor of Sangamon County. On May 7, 1833, Abraham Lincoln was appointed postmaster at the small town of New Salem.

Lincoln was a candidate for the legislature again in 1834 and was elected by a large majority. In the legislative session at Vandailia after his election, he sided with those who favored chartering a state bank, loaning money for canal building, and making internal improvements, but he remained silent during many of the deliberations.

Two years later he ran for a second term, and the election took place on the first Monday in August, 1836. Abraham Lincoln received a larger vote than any other candidate on the ballot. The two principal measures that were before the legislature in the 1836-1837 session were the internal improvement bill and the bill to relocate the state capital. Late in February, 1837, the internal improvement measure passed, and soon after this Springfield was selected as the state capital. Lincoln, as head of the nine-member Sangamon delegation, was influential in the selection of Springfield as the new seat of government.

Abraham Lincoln was elected to third term in the Illinois legislature in the 1838 election and went to Vandalia for the session that met on December 3, 1838. When the legislature adjourned on March 4, 1839, it marked the end of an era, since it was the last session held at Vandalia. The state records were moved to Springfield on July 4, 1839. In December of that year, the legislature met at Springfield for the first time. At the time of his last appearance in the legislature at Vandalia, in March, 1839, Abraham Lincoln was thirty years old. Since we are concerned in this volume with Vandalia as the capital of Illinois, we shall not follow the career of this great American after the move to Springfield.

After we drove through Bluff City, we soon crossed the Kaskaskia River at the edge of Vandalia, then went at once to the Vandalia Statehouse State Historic Site. The Vandalia Statehouse, and the public square surrounding it, were purchased in August, 1918, by the State of Illinois to make certain that they would be preserved for future generations. In a corner of the Statehouse grounds stands the sixth Madonna of the Trail Monument.

This monument was dedicated Friday, October 26, 1928, and a large crowd of people attended the ceremony.

The message on one side:

THE CUMBERLAND ROAD
BUILT BY
THE FEDERAL GOVERNMENT,
WAS AUTHORIZED BY CONGRESS
AND APPROVED BY
THOMAS JEFFERSON IN 1806.

VANDALIA MARKS THE
WESTERN TERMINUS.

The other message:

AT VANDALIA, ABRAHAM LINCOLN,
MEMBER OF ILLINOIS LEGISLATURE,
FIRST FORMULATED
THOSE BASIC HIGH PRINCIPLES
OF FREEDOM AND JUSTICE
WHICH GAVE THE SLAVES
A LIBERATOR,
THE UNION A SAVIOUR.

The original location of the Vandalia monument in 1928 was in front of the south entrance of the Statehouse, but it was moved to its present location at a later date. A rededication program was held on Saturday, November 4, 1978.

On the lawn near the monument, a metal plaque, mounted on a rough, irregular, whitish stone, gives a brief history of the Cumberland Road:

CUMBERLAND ROAD
VANDALIA WAS THE WESTERN TERMINUS
OF THE CUMBERLAND OR NATIONAL ROAD
WHICH EXTENDED EIGHTY FEET WIDE FOR
591 MILES FROM CUMBERLAND, MARYLAND
THROUGH PENNSYLVANIA, OHIO, INDIANA,
ILLINOIS. CONSTRUCTION BY THE
FEDERAL GOVERNMENT BEGAN IN 1811
AND CEASED IN 1838, THE APPROXIMATE
COST BEING SEVEN MILLION DOLLARS.

After our visit to Vandalia, we continued southwesterly and entered Bond County, founded January 4, 1817, and given the name of the first governor of Illinois, Shadrach Bond. The town of Mulberry Grove is situated just west of the county boundary, and we continued from here to Greenville. For three years (1818-1821) Perryville was the county seat of Bond County. Greenville, a town that had its start in 1815, was made the seat of government during 1821, and has been the county seat since then. Pocahontas, a few miles southwest of Greenville, was started after the earliest settlers arrived in 1838. It became a stop for stagecoaches on the Cumberland Road.

After we left Pocahontas we soon were in one of the western counties of Illinois, bordered by the Mississippi River. Madison County was established by a proclamation of the territorial governor on September 14, 1812, and named for James Madison, President of the United States from 1809 to 1817. The city of Edwardsville is the county seat.

Highland was our first destination in this county. We knew that the Swiss poet, Heinrich Bosshard, was buried here. The first settlers arrived from Kentucky and North Carolina in 1804. In 1831 several Swiss immigrants settled in this prairie town east of St. Louis. During the years that followed, the community continued to grow as more people migrated from Switzerland and established their homes here. In 1851 Heinrich Bosshard, forty years old, arrived in Highland. He was born April 8, 1811, in Canton Zurich, Switzerland, and died in Highland April 3, 1877. The Bosshard Monument in Lindenthal Park is a memorial to this Swiss composer. There are two inscriptions on the monument: one is in English and the other is in his native language.

The town of St. Jacob is a few miles west of Highland. From there the highway continues to Troy. This city, settled early in the nineteenth century, was named for Troy, New York. The railroad was built through the area in 1888 and four years later the city was incorporated. Paul Simon, United States Senator from Illinois, 1985 to 1997, at one time was publisher of *The Troy Tribune*.

After we left Troy we continued to Collinsville, settled in 1817 and given the name of William Collins, one of the first settlers. This city, incorporated in 1872, is located on the border of Madison and St. Clair Counties, and is situated on high ground above the fertile plain that lies along the Mississippi River. This fertile plain or low-lying land is known as the American Bottom. It was given this name when it was part of the western boundary of the United States. This narrow plain, approximately 100 miles long, extends south from the vicinity of Alton, Illinois, to Chester, the county seat of Randolph County.

After our visit to Collinsvill
e we soon reached Cahokia Mounds State Historic Site. This site, with its many mounds, has been designated as a World Heritage Site. It is located a few miles west of Collinsville, in the American Bottom. There are more than sixty mounds here. The largest is Monk's Mound, with a base that is more than fourteen acres in extent, and an overall height of 100 feet. The Visitor Center, built a few years ago to replace an older and smaller one, is outstanding, and the displays and exhibits make a visit very worthwhile.

The boundary line between Madison and St. Clair Counties passes south of the center of Collinsville and proceeds west through the Cahokia Mounds site. At the time Governor St. Clair established St. Clair County on April 27, 1790, and named it for himself, the county included most of southwestern Illinois, and Kaskaskia was the county seat. Within the next quarter century the following sequence of events took place:

1. On October 5, 1795, the southern portion of St. Clair County became Randolph County, with Kaskaskia as the county seat. At a later date, in 1847, Chester was made the seat of county government and has remained so to the present time.
2. In 1795, the year Randolph was made a county, Cahokia became the county seat of St. Clair County.
3. In 1814, Belleville replaced Cahokia as the county seat of St. Clair County, a change that has been in effect since that time.

Our destination after we left the World Heritage Site was East St. Louis in St. Clair County. An earlier town, settled at this location in 1818, preceded East St. Louis, and the present city was incorporated in 1861.

After driving through here we followed the Interstate Highway and finished out trip through Illinois. As we crossed the bridge over the Mississippi River, we entered St. Louis, Missouri.

Maryland

Pennsylvania

West Virginia

Ohio

Indiana

Illinois

Missouri

Kansas

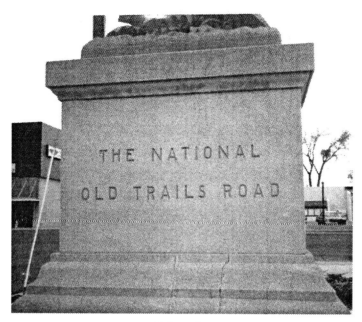

Colorado

New Mexico

Arizona

California

Chapter 8

Missouri

From the Missouri side of the bridge we had a close-up look at the Gateway Arch to our right. We had visited and stayed in St. Louis on previous trips, and on one of these we rode the tram to the observation deck at the top of this commemorative arch, an enjoyable experience. During another visit, we spent parts of two days in Forest Park in early May when the trees were alive with birds. The St. Louis Art Museum, with its nearby impressive statue of Saint Louis, was visited both days, allowing us enough time to see many works of art.

St. Louis was founded by the French fur trader Pierre Liguest Laclede. Born at Bedous, France, in 1724, he came to New Orleans, Louisiana, in 1755. Laclede came up the Mississippi River from New Orleans in 1763. After exploring the area, he selected the site on the west bank of the Mississippi where he wanted to build his trading post. In February, 1764, he sent Auguste Chouteau, thirteen years old, to the site with a group of workmen. They cleared the land and set up the first houses, built of logs. A few weeks later Pierre Laclede came to the settlement, carefully made a plan of his newly established village, and named it St. Louis. A few French settlers from east of the Mississippi River arrived later, and the village slowly began to grow.

On November 13, 1762, the King of France had given the entire colony of Louisiana to his cousin, the King of Spain, as a gift. This was not made public at the time, and it was in October, 1764, that it became known that Spain had gained control. In 1765, after the British sent troops to Illinois following the defeat of France in the French and Indian War, the population of St. Louis was increased when the French military commander and a number of his men moved there from Illinois.

For six years after St. Louis got its start, the French people were self-ruled, and in 1770 the first Spanish Commandant arrived.

In the next thirty years Spanish Commandants governed St. Louis, and the town grew from about 500 people in 1770, to a population of 925 in the last years of the eighteenth century. During the years of control by Spain, St. Louis continued as a French town and the Spanish population was small. The Spanish language was used for keeping official records, but French was the everyday language of most of the people.

By the late 1790s the French government had reason to believe that France might be able to get the Louisiana Territory back from Spain. Negotiations were started, and on October 1, 1800, the Treaty of Ildefonso was signed. Louisiana was a French colony again as it had been before the King gave it to Spain in 1762.

This set the stage for the next move that eventually more than doubled the area of the United States at that time. Within two years after Spain retroceded Louisiana to France in 1800, the French government was faced with the problem of protecting a large overseas colony against a strong England. Fearful that the latter might gain control of the mouth of the Mississippi River, and possibly all of Louisiana, France decided to sell this vast territory to the United States. After negotiations were completed, the treaty was signed on April 30, 1803, confirming the Louisiana Purchase, for $15,000,000. Nearly a year later, on March 10, 1804, at St. Louis, the Louisiana Territory officially was made a part of the United States. Major Amos Stoddard represented the United States, as the French flag was lowered and the Stars and Stripes took its place.

President Thomas Jefferson had decided soon after the Louisiana Purchase was ratified that this vast territory should be explored as soon as practicable. On May 14, 1804, Captain Meriwether Lewis and Captain William Clark left St. Louis at the head of an expedition that would take more than 28 months to complete, and would cover nearly 7,700 miles. Meriwether Lewis was born August 18, 1774, near Charlottesville, Virginia. By the time he was 21 years old he had gained military experience in the Virginia Militia at the time of the Whiskey Rebellion, and later, as a junior officer in the United States Army. He was well-acquainted with President Thomas Jefferson and was his personal secretary in 1801 and 1802.

William Clark, four years older than Meriwether Lewis, was born August 1, 1770, in Caroline County, Virginia. He was a younger brother of General George Rogers Clark of Revolutionary War fame. William Clark also had military training before he was 21 years old, on expeditions against Indians and while defending Kentucky settlements. On March 7, 1792, he was commissioned lieutenant in the regular army, and following this served under General Anthony Wayne. When President Jefferson asked Meriwether Lewis to lead the exploration, Lewis selected William Clark to be co-leader of the expedition.

The explorers traveled slowly up the Missouri River and on May 16 reached St. Charles. Continuing westward up the Missouri they set up their camps at suitable sites and became acquainted with the Indian tribes along their route, trading with them on occasion. On June 26, 1804, they camped at the mouth of the Kansas River and stayed there for three days. From this point their route was more northerly as they continued to follow the Missouri River. By early August they were at Council Bluffs, Iowa, across the river from Omaha, Nebraska.

The expedition spent the winter of 1804-1805 at Fort Mandan in what is now North Dakota. Early in April, 1805, they headed westward. Seven months later, on November 7, 1805, they reached the Oregon coast where they stayed until spring, after they had built Fort Clatsop on a site a few miles south of the Columbia River. Their journey back to St. Louis took six months, from March 23 to September 23, 1806. They had accomplished all that could be expected of them, having learned much about the Indians, the climate, and the flora and fauna. They also brought back knowledge concerning the topographical features of the Louisiana Purchase and of the country on west to the Pacific Ocean.

On March 3, 1807, President Jefferson appointed Meriwether Lewis as the governor of Louisiana Territory. General James Wilkinson had been governor since his appointment by the President on March 11, 1805. Soon after Meriwether Lewis was named governor, William Clark became Indian agent for Louisiana Territory. Clark also was designated as the commanding officer of the territorial militia. In September, 1809, Governor Lewis left Louisiana Territory to return to Washington, D. C., in order to clear up some misunderstandings concerning his activities as governor of the territory. On October 11, 1809, at the age of 35, Meriwether Lewis died suddenly in Tennessee under mysterious circumstances. There have always been unanswered questions concerning the cause of his death.

The population of Missouri grew slowly after the Louisiana Purchase, and there was a question concerning which town would be the center of business and political activity. The town of Ste. Genevieve on the Mississippi River, south of St. Louis, rivaled the latter for a few years, but St. Louis began steady growth and became the seat of government.

In 1808 three events that were important in the development of St. Louis took place. In that year the town was incorporated, making it the first incorporated town in Missouri and also the first west of the Mississippi River; the first newspaper west of the Mississippi was published; the first public territorial road was established by the territorial legislature, from St. Louis through Ste. Genevieve and Cape Girardeau, to New Madrid, following in a general way the Mississippi River. The road was opened in 1813.

On April 30, 1812, the Territory of Orleans was admitted to the Union as the State of Louisiana, and became the 18th state. This was nine years after Ohio entered the Union in 1803, as the 17th state. An Act of Congress on June 4, 1812, changed the name of the Territory of Louisiana, and it became the Territory of Missouri. This Act set up a government for the new territory, with a General Assembly that consisted of the Governor, a Legislative Council of nine members, and a House of Representatives. William Clark became governor of the Territory of Missouri, July 1, 1813, and held that position for the remainder of the territorial years.

The War of 1812 slowed the growth and development of Missouri Territory. The Treaty of Ghent, signed late in December, 1814, officially ended the war, and, in the next six years, the population of the territory increased from about 25, 000 to more than 65, 000 in 1820. Prior to the end of the war, most of the population of Missouri Territory lived in the areas that bordered the Mississippi River, from St. Louis south to New Madrid. With the coming of peace, thousands of people from states east of the Mississippi pushed toward the west and settled where they could find vacant land. Many of these followed the Missouri River and established settlements adjacent to this great waterway.

St. Louis, the territorial capital, had grown steadily, and by 1818 was becoming a busy center of population on the frontier. Early in August, 1817, the steamboat *Zebulon M. Pike* docked at St. Louis. This was the first time a steamboat had proceeded up the Mississippi River to a point north of the Ohio River. Within two years steamboats were making regular stops at St. Louis, but steamboat travel on the Missouri River was not commonplace until nearly ten years later.

As the population of Missouri Territory increased, the territorial legislature established new counties to administer the newly settled area. On March 16, 1818, the Missouri delegate to Congress presented a petition requesting statehood for the territory. There was extended debate in Congress concerning the admission of Missouri as a state. While this was being decided in the nation's capital, the territorial authorities proceeded with the organization of a state government. An election was held on August 28, 1820, and Alexander McNair was elected governor, defeating William Clark who had been governor during the territorial years preceding statehood. William Clark lived in Missouri the rest of his life and was 68 years old when he died on September 1, 1838, at St. Louis.

The first General Assembly met in St. Louis on September 18, 1820, and a commission of five men was appointed to select a site for the state capital. The commission was instructed to find a location on the Missouri River, and finally, on December 31, 1821, the present site of Jefferson City was selected. St. Charles became the state capital until October 1, 1826, during which time the statehouse and other facilities were built at the new settlement of Jefferson City. The first house had been built here in 1819.

The capital city was named for Thomas Jefferson, President of the United States at the time of the Louisiana Purchase. President James Monroe issued a proclamation, August 10, 1821, stating that Missouri was admitted to the Union as the 24th state.

Our route after we entered Missouri took us through the city of St. Louis to Wellston, then continued through the western section of St. Louis County to the Missouri River. One of the original counties of Missouri, St. Louis County was organized October 1, 1812. The city of Clayton, not on our route, is the county seat. After we crossed the Missouri, we entered the city of St. Charles, county seat of St. Charles County, another of the five original counties that were established in October, 1812.

This city, about twenty miles northwest of St. Louis, was settled late in the eighteenth century but growth was slow until the Lewis and Clark Expedition returned from the west in 1806. Within two years many houses were built, as well as supply shops and several stores. On October 13, 1809, a village organization was established, and nearly forty years later St. Charles was incorporated as a city on March 10, 1849.

The Missouri River forms the southern boundary of St. Charles County. This county extends east to the point where the Missouri enters the Mississippi River.

We left St. Charles via the highway that took us southwest to the community of Harvester, then in a few miles turned to the northwest to the village of Cottleville, named for Lorenzo Cottle, born September 13, 1811. Early in 1831 he enlisted for service in the Black Hawk War and served for a year. In 1837 he was again in uniform as a member of the Missouri volunteers in action against the Seminole Indians in Florida. When this tour of duty was over, he resumed farming in St. Charles County.

After a brief stop in Cottleville we continued to Wentzville, named in honor of the chief railroad engineer who directed the survey and layout of the town in 1855. Wentzville has grown to a population of about 5,000 or more inhabitants. Beyond Wentzville we came to the village of Foristell, laid out two years after Wentzville and originally called Snow Hill, but changed to Foristell in 1877.

Warren County, organized January 5, 1833, was entered just west of Foristell. The Missouri River bounds this county at the south as it does St. Charles County. Our first town in Warren County was Wright City, the birthplace of the author and lecturer, Reinhold

Niebuhr. Niebuhr was born June 21, 1892, and died at Stockbridge, Massachusetts, on June 1, 1971. He received the Medal of Freedom from President Lyndon B. Johnson in 1964.

West of Wright City is the village of Truesdale, situated about two miles to the east of Warrenton. Warrenton has been the county seat of Warren County since 1836, and both Warren County and Warrenton were named for General Joseph Warren. Joseph Warren was born at Roxbury, Massachusetts, near Boston, on June 11, 1741. Trained as a physician, he had a medical practice in Boston and became active in the political affairs of Massachusetts prior to the War for Independence. Early in 1775 he was placed in charge of a commission to organize an army in Massachusetts. General Warren died instantly during the Battle of Bunker Hill on June 17, 1775, when he was shot by one of the British soldiers attacking the American position.

We drove into Jonesburg, a village that received the name of James Jones, who came from North Carolina and settled here late in the 1820s. Although a small settlement developed during the following years, Jonesburg was not laid out until 1858, after the railroad came through the area.

We were now in Montgomery County, established December 14, 1818. The name of this county honors General Richard Montgomery, killed at the Battle of Quebec, as described previously in the Montgomery County, Ohio segment. The county seat of Montgomery County, Missouri, has been Montgomery City since 1924. We passed through the towns of High Hill and New Florence on our way to Danville, named for Danville, Virginia. Danville was made the county seat of Montgomery County in 1834, and was a prosperous community until the Civil War, when a raiding party destroyed much of the town.

After we left Danville, we continued to Mineola, then on west to Williamsburg, a town laid out in 1837. The county boundary between Montgomery and Callaway Counties is a few miles west of Danville, and the 357-acre Graham Cave State Park is situated just east of this boundary. The organization of Callaway County took place on November 25, 1820. It was named in remembrance of Captain James Callaway. The Captain was killed March 7, 1815, in a battle with Indians. At a road junction several miles west of Williamsburg, we took a road to the southwest through the village of Calwood, then to Fulton. Five years after Callaway County was organized, Fulton was named the county seat in June, 1825. The town was first named Volney, but later the name was changed to Fulton, in memory of Robert Fulton whose steamboat successfully made the trip up the Hudson River in August, 1807.

The Winston Churchill Memorial and Library, on the campus of Westminster College in Fulton, commemorates the achievements of this statesman who led England through the trying years of World War II. It was at Westminster College that Winston Churchill delivered his famous "Iron Curtain" speech on March 5, 1946. The displays of documents and other Churchill memorabilia make a visit here very worthwhile. Outside the building at the top of the steps is a statue of this wartime leader, with the single word, CHURCHILL, inscribed near the top of the base.

From Fulton we traveled northwest to Millersburg, and soon entered Boone County, established November 16, 1820. This is one of several counties in the United States that is named for Daniel Boone. In a short time we were in the city of Columbia. This city had its beginning in 1819 and received its present name two years later. Within a short time it was made the county seat of Boone County, and in 1826 was incorporated.

In the 1830s many people of Missouri became interested in founding a state university. On June 4, 1839, a commission authorized by the state legislature selected Boone County as the home of a university that would be established by using the proceeds of a land grant made by Congress. Boone County had subscribed the largest total of funds in support of the university of any county in the state. The cornerstone of the university was laid at the site in Columbia on July 4, 1840. Courses began at the University of Missouri on April 14, 1841. Missouri was the first state west of the Mississippi River to establish a state university.

West of Columbia, the highway we were following passed through the village of Midway, then intersected a road that goes southeast to Rocheport, situated on the north bank of the Missouri River, about one mile from the intersection. A ferry was in operation at Rocheport in 1819, and the village was laid out in 1825. We returned to the main highway, then continued to the west nearly ten miles and turned to the north a short distance into New Franklin. A sign here stated:

City Limit
NEW FRANKLIN
Pop. 1107

Several miles east of New Franklin we had entered Howard County on our way from Columbia.

After the War of 1812 ended, the population of Missouri increased rapidly, as we have noted. Howard County was created January 13, 1816, and in that year the town of Franklin, named after Benjamin Franklin, was founded on the Missouri River. From its start Franklin grew rapidly and in 1817 was made the county seat of Howard County. In 1823, Fayette became the county seat, and has remained the seat of county government since then.

Within three years after Franklin was settled, there were more than one hundred log houses and several frame houses, at least a dozen stores, and various other businesses. One of these was a printing office that issued a weekly newspaper. The latter began publication on April 23, 1819, and was the first newspaper to be published west of St. Louis.

It was in this Franklin newspaper that William Becknell published an advertisement in June, 1821. Little is known about Becknell's early life, but he was born about 1790 and may have spent part of his childhood in Kentucky, then arrived in Missouri. He was a veteran of the War of 1812 and afterward lived in Howard County. In his advertisement he asked for men to join him for a trip to the southwest Rocky Mountains, and a sufficient number of volunteers responded.

Preparations were made during the next few weeks and a stock of trading goods was loaded on mules prior to departure. The party crossed the Missouri River at Arrow Rock, several miles northwest of Franklin, September 1, 1821. On November 16, after an arduous journey, they reached Santa Fe, New Mexico, and were received hospitably by the Mexican population. Here they were able to sell at a profit the goods brought from Missouri. Near the middle of December, William Becknell left Sante Fe and arrived back in Franklin on January 29, 1822.

Prior to the Becknell trip to Santa Fe, a number of Americans had been in this town in New Mexico. There is a record of an American citizen who arrived in this Mexican town during June, 1805, and found employment that afforded him a good living. In March, 1807, Lt. Zebulon Pike, for whom Pikes Peak was named, reached Santa Fe with his party of explorers. They were detained by Spanish authorities, then sent to Chihuahua, Mexico. Subsequently, Pike and his men were released and sent back to the United States through present-day Texas. In 1810, three Americans, who may have been on a trading trip, were stopped by Spanish troops, taken to Santa Fe, then imprisoned in Mexico for two years.

In May, 1822, several months after Becknell returned to Franklin, he left on a second trip to Santa Fe. In his small caravan he had three wagons loaded with trading goods, more merchandise than could be packed by several mules. He changed the route on this second trip by turning to the southwest at a point beyond present-day Dodge City, Kansas, and traveling across country that later was known as the Cimarron Desert. This route avoided some of the mountain travel he had experienced the year before. Becknell has been called the Father of the Santa Fe Trail, and this is justified. His trips opened the trail to Santa Fe as a profitable commercial route to the west. In the half-century or so afterward, many caravans and thousands of people followed the Santa Fe Trail. Thus this route to the west played an important part in the westward expansion of our nation.

William Becknell remained active in Missouri after the initial trips described above. In 1824, he led a caravan of more than twenty wagons from Independence, Missouri, to Santa Fe. Four years after this, he founded a ferry service across the Missouri River at Arrow Rock. Later he was a member of the state legislature of Missouri, then left Missouri and moved to Texas. Becknell was active in Texas at the time this future state became independent from Mexico and was admitted to the Union as the 28th state. At a later date, he established his home in northeastern Texas. William Becknell died in 1865.

By the early 1820s, the population of Franklin exceeded 1,000 inhabitants, and several well-known Missourians called this town their home. Two men of widely different occupations spent their youthful years in Franklin, then became known beyond the borders of Missouri.

Christopher (Kit) Carson was born December 24, 1809, in Madison County, Kentucky, the fifth of ten children. In 1811, when Kit was less than two years old, the family moved to the Franklin-Arrow Rock area of Missouri. At some time in 1818, Kit's father was killed when a tree limb fell on him. Kit never attended school, and in 1825 his mother arranged with a saddlemaker in Franklin to take Kit into the shop as an apprentice. The next year, a few months before he was seventeen years old, Kit ran away and hired out as a worker on a caravan headed for Santa Fe, New Mexico. Within a few years he became an experienced trapper and guide. In the 1840s, John C. Fremont selected him as a guide on the exploring expeditions that he led. During the 1850s, he was appointed as a United States Indian Agent and was in this post for more than seven years. When the Civil War started, he resigned this position, and as a colonel was in charge of troops in the Battle of Valverde, New Mexico. He was active in campaigns against Indian tribes in 1863 and 1864, and in 1866 was in command of Fort Garland in western Colorado. Kit Carson's health failed and he died at Fort Lyon, Colorado, on May 23, 1868, and was buried in Taos, New Mexico.

George Caleb Bingham was born in Augusta County, Virginia, March 20, 1811. His family moved to Franklin in 1819, when he was eight years old. Bingham was a self-taught artist while working at different jobs and took up portrait painting while quite young. By 1834, when he was 23 years old, he had decided to make art his lifework. In 1837 or 1838 he had an opportunity to study at the Pennsylvania Academy of Fine Arts for a short time.

From 1840 to 1844, Caleb Bingham lived in Washington, D. C., and he was in Europe for about three years in the 1850s. He was acquainted with other states of the United States, but the state of Missouri was his home. Bingham moved his studio several times;

it was located at Columbia, Arrow Rock, St. Louis, Jefferson City, and Kansas City during his career. George Caleb Bingham died at Kansas City, Missouri, on July 7, 1879.

Franklin prospered for several years after the Santa Fe trade began, but later in the decade of the 1820s the floodwater of the Missouri River washed away most of the town. In 1828, the town of New Franklin was laid out. Many residents of Franklin moved to the new town, situated on higher ground, about two miles away. By the time Franklin had dropped into the Missouri River the starting place for the trade with Santa Fe had moved to western Missouri.

After visiting New Franklin we crossed the Missouri River on a steel bridge high above the water and entered Boonville, first settled in 1810. This city is the county seat of Cooper County, organized December 17, 1818. Going west out of Boonville, we came to Lamine, then followed the road to Arrow Rock in Saline County.

Laid out on May 23, 1829, and called New Philadelphia for a few years, the name of the town was changed to Arrow Rock. Many years before the town was founded, this site was important as a place to cross the Missouri River. A natural stone marker stands near the highway and gives this information:

SANTA FE TRAIL
1822-1872
Marked by the
Daughters of the
American Revolution
and the
State of Missouri
1909
ARROW ROCK

The village of Hardeman was on our route after we left Arrow Rock and in a few miles we came to Marshall, the county seat of Saline County. Settlers first arrived here in 1839, and the town they started was named for John Marshall, for whom Marshall, Illinois, also was named. This statesman was appointed Secretary of State by President John Adams in 1800, and the next year became a member of the United States Supreme Court, where he served for 34 years, as shown previously in the Illinois segment of this volume. Saline County was organized November 25, 1820, and received its name because of the many salt springs in the area. The state route that brought us to Marshall has been named the Lewis and Clark Trail.

The town of Malta Bend, west of Marshall, was laid out in 1867, and named for the *Malta*, a Missouri River steamboat that sank in 1841 in the bend of the river that is north of the townsite. Less than five miles farther west brought us to Grand Pass. This small village got its name from the ridge, or narrow elevation, between the valleys of the Missouri River and the nearby creek. This higher ground formed a natural east-west route south of the Missouri River.

We soon reached the town of Waverly, located on the southern bank of the Missouri. Established in 1845, it received its present name in 1848. Between Grand Pass and Waverly we had crossed the boundary between Saline and Lafayette Counties. As noted on a previous page, several counties in the United States are named Lafayette, after the Marquis de Lafayette of France. This county was created November 16, 1820, and the next year was called Lillard County. By an Act on February 16, 1825, the legislature changed the name to Lafayette.

For the next thirty miles west of Waverly, our route closely followed the Missouri River and was seldom more than two miles or so south of it. Dover, a small village, was laid out in 1835 and was the second community that was settled in Lafayette County. As we traveled toward Lexington, we noted the many apple orchards and fruit stands in this section of Missouri.

A ferry was started in 1819 at the site of Lexington, and soon a community developed here. In 1822 the town was laid out and given its present name. Many of the pioneers had come from Kentucky, a number of them from Lexington in that state. The new town was made the county seat of Lafayette County in 1823, and soon became a thriving business center on the Missouri River.

There are many cities and towns in the United States that are called Lexington and their names stem directly or indirectly from Lexington, Massachusetts. It was here that a small body of American minutemen confronted a much larger force of British soldiers on April 19, 1775. This encounter was the opening battle of the long War for Independence.

In addition to the county seat of Lafayette County, Missouri, there are eight other counties in the United States with Lexington as the county seat.

During the Civil War, another Battle of Lexington was fought, nearly a century after the opening shots of the American Revolution at Lexington, Massachusetts. This was the three-day battle fought at Lexington, Missouri, on September 18, 19, 20, 1861. This conflict between Union and Confederate forces is commemorated at the Battle of Lexington State Historic Site, and we enjoyed our visit here.

The seventh Madonna of the Trail Monument is located at Lexingon in a small park near the Missouri River. Close to this monument stands a low stone with a Santa Fe Trail inscription mounted on one surface. The wording of the inscription is very similar to that of the natural stone Santa Fe Trail marker at Arrow Rock. This was described earlier. Several feet from the low stone, a sign is suspended from a pole:

HISTORIC
LEXINGTON

MADONNA
of the
TRAIL
1928

Dedication ceremonies for this Madonna Monument were held on Monday, September 17, 1928. A half century later, on September 20, 1978, this monument was rededicated.

The inscription on one panel of the monument has this message:

LEXINGTON
SETTLED 1820 BY
VIRGINIA AND KENTUCKY
PIONEERS.
EARLY TERMINUS OF
RIVER TRANSPORTATION,
STARTING POINT ON THE
WESTERN TRAIL OF THE
PACK PONY AND OX CART

On the other panel the inscription reads:

JOHN, JAMES AND ROBERT AULL
RUSSELL MAJORS & WADDEL
DONIPHAN
PIONEERS — TRADERS
SOLDIERS — CITIZENS
OF LEXINGTON
WHO GAVE VALIANT SERVICE
TO THE WINNING OF THE WEST

After our visit to Lexington we soon came to the town of Wellington, and a few miles farther on we entered Jackson County. This county on the western border of Missouri was founded December 15, 1826, and named for Andrew Jackson, the General who led American forces to victory in the Battle of New Orleans during the War of 1812. Andrew Jackson became the seventh President of the United States and served two terms, 1829-1837.

We drove through the village of Levasy and soon arrived at Buckner, a town started in 1875 after the railroad was built through the area. Several miles west of Buckner, we crossed the Little Blue River and stopped at a roadside plaque with a Jackson County, Missouri, emblem at the top. The title of the plaque was: ENGAGEMENT AT THE LITTLE BLUE. It told of the battle between Confederate and Union forces on October 21, 1864. After leaving here we soon entered the city of Independence.

In 1825, settlers arrived at the site of Independence. After Jackson County was established late the following year, the town was laid out and was made the county seat in 1827. By the last years of the 1820s, most of the caravans going to Santa Fe started from Independence. Beginning in 1850, monthly mail service was in effect between Independence and Santa Fe.

By the late 1830s and during the 1840s and 1850s, Independence became the starting place for wagon trains going to the Oregon country, as thousands of pioneers made the long journey to the Northwest over the Oregon Trail.

Harry S Truman, the thirty-third President of the United States, was born at Lamar, Missouri, May 8, 1884. He grew up in the Independence-Kansas City area, attended school in Independence and graduated from high school there in 1901. During the next few years he worked at various jobs in Independence and Kansas City. After 1906, and until the United States entered World War I, work on the family farm near Kansas City took much of his time.

In the first World War, Harry Truman saw action in France as a commissioned officer. Soon after his return in 1919, Truman and Bess Wallace were married and established their home in Independence. He was selected as a judge of the Jackson County Court in 1922, but in 1924 was not reelected. This was the only defeat at the polls that he ever experienced. In 1926, he won election to the county court again and served as presiding judge until he was elected to the U.S. Senate in 1934. In 1928 and 1929, Judge Truman gave an address at several dedication programs for the Madonna of the Trail Monuments.

After his six-year term in the Senate, he was reelected in 1940. In 1944 he was nominated as the Democratic candidate for vice-president, and won the election as the running mate of Franklin D. Roosevelt. When President Roosevelt died on April 12, 1945, Harry S Truman became President of the United States. In 1948, he was elected to the office and served until January 20, 1953, when Dwight D. Eisenhower took office as the thirty-fourth President of the United States.

The Harry S Truman Library in Independence was completed in 1957. With its untold thousands of papers and documents, the library is administered as a research center, used by scholars from the United States and other parts of the world. The adjoining museum is devoted to the life and presidency of this man who served his country for many years. On display are the replica of the Truman White House office and items that depict the history of the United States in the years that followed World War II.

The home where Harry S Truman and his wife lived is located only a few blocks from the library and museum. A sign in the yard, "Truman House," gives a brief history of the home and states that it was the "Summer White House" during the years of the Truman presidency. The house and surrounding district are designated as the Harry S Truman National Historic Site.

From the time he left Washington, after his years as senator, vice-president, and president, President Harry S Truman and his wife continued to live in this house in Independence.

President Truman died in Kansas City, Missouri, on December 26, 1972, at the age of 88 years. Mrs. Truman outlived her husband by nearly ten years, and died October 18, 1982, at age 97. Their graves are in the courtyard of the Harry S Truman Library.

By the 1840s, Independence had lost some of the Missouri River traffic and business that it gained after the disastrous flood at Franklin, prior to 1830. Steamboat captains had found that several miles up the river from Independence a rock ledge extended into the Missouri from the south bank. This was a suitable place to tie up and unload their cargoes. At this point, about a mile below the confluence of the Missouri and Kansas Rivers, a trading post had been established in 1821. In 1834, the town of Westport was laid out in the prairie four miles south of this levee. After a road was built from Westport, this was named Westport Landing.

Independence continued to outfit caravans for the western trails and was the leading source of equipment for many years, but Westport and its Landing began to increase their share of the business. By starting from Westport, caravans could save a day or so of travel on the outbound trip, with a similar saving when they returned.

Kansas City, Missouri, had its beginning at Westport Landing in late 1838, when land was purchased as the site for the Town of Kansas. The site included frontage on the south bank of the Missouri River, at the Landing, and the acreage extended south of the river. In the spring of 1839, lots in the new town were surveyed and some were sold. The location of the Town of Kansas, near the place where the Missouri River turns to the north, made it a transfer point for many of those who came up the Missouri and started overland on the Santa Fe and Oregon Trails.

By 1848, ten years after the town was started, it was growing steadily, and more caravans and wagon trains made this their headquarters. A charter was obtained in February, 1853, and the town was incorporated March 28, 1853. In 1865, a railroad from the east entered the Town of Kansas, and in 1869 a railroad bridge was built across the Missouri River. This assured the future of the town as a transportation center. As the Town of Kansas grew, its name became City of Kansas, then, increasingly, it was called Kansas City. Its growth to the south absorbed Westport, and a large area north of the Missouri River became part of the city.

The dividing line between Kansas City, Missouri, and its counterpart in the state of Kansas is a street, State Line Road. The Missouri River forms the boundary farther north. Kansas City, Missouri, is the larger of the two cities, whose metropolitan areas extend into several counties of the two states. The two Kansas Cities are politically separate, but, together, make up the Greater Kansas City area.

On other trips prior to this one, we had been in Kansas City. After the short drive from Independence, we spent part of the day there, then entered Kansas.

Chapter 9

Kansas

The state of Kansas became part of the United States as a result of the Louisiana Purchase. Long before the first explorers arrived here, Kansas was inhabited by a number of Indian tribes, with a population of many thousands.

The Arapahoe, Cheyenne, and Kiowa were among the wandering tribes that made the area their home. On a smaller scale, other tribes such as the Apaches made trips into Kansas to hunt or to make war. The Kansa, Pawnee, and Osage tribes were more representative of the Indian way of living on the Plains of Kansas. Many members of these tribes lived in villages, cultivated crops, and were hunters of buffalo and smaller animals for food.

From the earliest years of colonization on the eastern coast of our country, Indians had been placed on reservations or were forced to move westward as the colonists took over the land. Before the middle of the nineteenth century, this policy had resulted in the emigration of the Delaware, Shawnee, and Wyandot Indians into Kansas from the east.

In the 1830s, many people crossed Kansas on the Santa Fe Trail; by the 1840s, both the Santa Fe and Oregon Trails were used by thousands. The number of settlers in Kansas at that time was very small. Most of the sparse population lived in settlements near trading posts and near the forts that were maintained on the frontier by the military.

In 1842, the United States Government authorized exploring expeditions to the Rocky Mountains, Oregon, and California under the Army officer, John C. Fremont. The first trip started in June of that year from a trading post on the Kansas River and explored parts of present-day Kansas, Nebraska, Colorado, and Wyoming. He finished the trip early in October, 1842.

Late in May, 1843, Fremont started from Kansas on a second exploration that took his party to Idaho, Utah, Oregon, Nevada, and California. This trip ended on the last day of July, 1844.

The published reports of these explorations brought fame to Fremont, and knowledge of the West to the public. In 1845 and 1847, Fremont led his third and fourth expeditions, both to California.

Gold was discovered in California late in January, 1848, and word of the discovery reached the East coast some weeks later. In 1849 and 1850, the years of the gold rush, a conservative estimate of 50,000 or more travelers crossed Kansas each year. All of this travel had little permanent effect on the population of Kansas, as only a small number of the travelers decided to stay in Kansas instead of proceeding to California.

Over a period of years, Indian tribes in Kansas, by a series of treaties, ceded their land to the United States Government. In exchange for giving up their land, many of the Indians agreed to leave the area and move to the Indian Territory in Oklahoma. A number of those who were displaced acquired land and remained in Kansas as farmers. In the spring of 1854, the Delaware and Shawnee tribes, with reservations in eastern Kansas, signed treaties that gave up most of their acreage. Thousands of people from states east of the Mississippi River, and from Missouri, swarmed across the boundary into Kansas to buy the hundreds of square miles of land that were available for settlement.

On May 30, 1854, President Franklin Pierce signed the Kansas-Nebraska bill that created Kansas Territory and Nebraska Territory. The northern, eastern, and southern boundaries of Kansas Territory were the boundaries of the present state of Kansas. The western boundary of this large territory was the "east boundary of the Territory of Utah, on the summit of the Rocky Mountains."

The population of the Territory of Kansas increased rapidly after the events that occurred in 1854. By 1860, the census exceeded 100,000 people as farms were established, and many villages and towns were founded in the counties that were organized farther to the west.

On January 29, 1861, President James Buchanan signed the bill that admitted Kansas to the Union as the 34th state. The boundaries of the state on the north, east, and south remained as they had been as a territory, but in the words of the Act of Admission, "thence west on said parallel to the twenty-fifth meridian of longitude west from Washington; thence north on said meridian to the fortieth parallel of latitude." In February, 1861, the western section of the Territory of Kansas became part of the Territory of Colorado.

Records show that the elevation above sea level in the state varies from 680 feet in Montgomery County, in the southeast corner, to 4,039 feet at the top of Mount Sunflower in Wallace County, near the Kansas-Colorado state line. The average change of elevation, from the lowest point in the east to the highest point in the west, is about nine feet per mile, but the change is not constant. There are areas that are level and some that are hilly. Rivers and creeks throughout the state flow through valleys that comprise drainage areas of varying sizes. The geographical center of the 48 conterminous states of the United States is in Smith County, Kansas, at a point about thirteen miles south of the Kansas-Nebraska state line.

After Kansas became part of the Union on January 29, 1861, it was nearly a year before the permanent location of the state capital was decided. An election was held on November 5, 1861, and Topeka received the most votes. Topeka had been founded December 5, 1854, several months after Kansas was made a territory, and was incorporated in 1857.

Wyandotte County, situated immediately west of Kansas City, Missouri, was established January 29, 1859. It has the smallest land area of any county in Kansas, with 149 square miles. Kansas City, Kansas, the county seat of Wyandotte County, had its beginning in 1868, when a town company was organized by several businessmen from Missouri. Within a few years after that, several other towns were started in the vicinity. In the 1880s, these small towns began to merge and eventually the Kansas City, Kansas, of the present day developed.

Our route as we came into Kansas was through the southeastern corner of Wyandotte County and into Johnson County. This county was one of several counties that were established by the legislature in August, 1855, and was named for the missionary, Thomas Johnson. We spent some time in the cities of Shawnee, Overland Park and Lenexa, all of which are part of the Greater Kansas City area.

A sign that we noted pertained to the early history of this site
on the Santa Fe Trail:

SANTA FE
TRAIL
HISTORIC SITE
Original site of
GUM SPRINGS
Sign courtesy of
SHAWNEE
HISTORICAL SOCIETY

We drove to the southwest and in a few miles came to Olathe,
the county seat of Johnson County. The founders of the town decided that the Shawnee Indian word, *olathe*, described the beautiful and pleasing locality they had selected. On February 20, 1857,
the Olathe Town Company was incorporated, and the Act that incorporated Olathe as a city was passed by the Territorial Legislature during the session that adjourned February 13, 1858.

Continuing in the same direction after we left Olathe, we
reached Gardner, named for one of the founders of the town. The
first settlers arrived here in 1857. The Santa Fe and Oregon Trails
followed the same route for a number of miles in eastern Kansas.
At a point about two miles west of Gardner, they separated, and
the trail to Santa Fe continued to the west. The Oregon Trail made
a turn to the right and headed toward the northwest.

At the town of Edgerton, a few miles from Gardner, the highway we are following turned more directly west from its southwesterly trend, and we soon entered Douglas County. This was
another of the counties established in August, 1855, by the first
territorial legislature. It was named for Senator Stephan A. Douglas of Illinois. It was Senator Douglas who introduced and sponsored the Kansas-Nebraska bill that created the two territories. In
1858, the Lincoln-Douglas debates took place in Illinois, and there
is little doubt that the result of these had an influence on the national election two years later.

110

After about ten miles we came to Baldwin City, named for John Baldwin who came from Ohio in 1857. Originally named Baldwin, on February 11, 1859, it was incorporated as a city by the Territorial Legislature, and thus became Baldwin City.

Beyond Baldwin City we drove through the small village of Worden. Then, about a dozen miles farther on, we entered Osage County. This county was established on February 11, 1859, when the legislature changed Weller County to Osage County. After we crossed the Osage County boundary we came to Overbrook. The name of this town may have come from Pennsylvania to Kansas, as there is a town near Philadelphia that is named Overbrook. Soon after Overbrook, we arrived at Scranton, named for Scranton, Pennsylvania, then continued several miles to Burlingame, a town that was named Council City after it was founded. The name of the town was changed to its present name in 1870, in honor of Anson Burlingame of Massachusetts. Anson Burlingame was a member of Congress from 1856 to 1861 as a Representative from Massachusetts. From 1861 to 1867, he was the United States Minister to China during the administrations of Presidents Abraham Lincoln and Andrew Johnson. At the conclusion of his term as minister in 1867 until his death in 1870, he was employed by the Chinese government to negotiate treaties with other countries.

At Burlingame our road turned to the south for several miles, then headed west again. Soon after we made the turn to the west, we turned left (south) on the road that took us to Osage City, about one mile away. At the time it was founded, this town was named Osage, like the county, but the Post Office Department gave it the present name by adding the word "city." After our brief visit here, we returned to our original route and continued to the west, then entered Lyon County.

This county was created February 5, 1862, and named for an officer of the Union army, Nathaniel Lyon. General Lyon was killed August 10, 1861, at the Battle of Wilson's Creek in southern Missouri. Admire, a small town on our route through Lyon County, received the name of Jacob V. Admire, another Union officer who served in the Civil War. He was the captain of a company of Indiana infantry, and made Kansas his home after the war. Here he became a lawyer and newspaperman and was elected to the state legislature. Jacob V. Admire died at Enid, Oklahoma, in 1911.

A few more miles brought us to the village of Allen, whose name was derived from the first name of Allen McGee. McGee was authorized as a contractor to construct buildings on Indian land. Later he was a licensed trader with the Indians.

Soon we drove through the small town of Bushong, originally named Weeks, for Joseph Weeks. At the time the railroad was being surveyed and built through Lyon County in the latter part of the nineteenth century, Weeks donated land so a station could be built here. The name was changed to Bushong at a later date. In a few miles we were out of Lyon County, then entered Morris County. This county was originally established by the territorial legislature in 1855, and was named Wise. Four years later, on February 11, 1859, the legislature changed the name to Morris. This honored Thomas Morris, elected to the United States Senate from Ohio. Within a few miles we came to Council Grove, the county seat of Morris County.

The early history of Council Grove was closely related to the history of the Santa Fe Trail. On August 10, 1825, less than four years after William Becknell left Franklin, Missouri, on his first trip to Santa Fe, a treaty was signed at Council Grove. At a meeting between the chiefs of the Osage Indian tribe and three U.S. Government Commissioners, the government promised a monetary payment to the tribe. In return, the Osage Indians gave the United States the right to survey and use the road to Santa Fe. The grove where the council was held and the treaty was signed was part of a large stand of timber near the Neosho River. Early in the present century, it was stated at Council Grove that "for ages (this) has been, and still is, the largest body of natural timber from here to the Rocky Mountains."

Within a few years after the treaty of 1825, many wagon trains starting from Independence or Westport, Missouri, stopped at Council Grove on their way to Santa Fe. At this place wagons could ford the Neosho River, where the banks sloped to the water and the river bed had a solid bottom. The caravans were now more than 100 miles west of their starting place, a journey of perhaps eight or ten days, and they could rest, feed and water their animals, and could repair their wagons with the available supply of timber. Parties returning from Santa Fe also stopped here after their long journey.

The settlement grew very slowly during the two decades that followed the treaty. By 1847 a store had been opened and a stock of goods was made available to travelers on the Santa Fe Trail. Before the decade ended, several houses were built, and one or two blacksmith shops were in the wagon repair business. The settlement was incorporated as a town by the territorial legislature that adjourned February 11, 1859.

The memory of the Santa Fe Trail is kept alive in Council Grove. The part that remains of the Council Oak where the treaty was signed is preserved for present and future generations. There are records that indicate that the tree was still alive and flourishing in 1903, and that it was still standing until destroyed by the wind in 1958.

About a block away is the Post Office Oak, marked with a nearby sign:

POST OFFICE OAK
FROM 1825 TO 1847
A CACHE AT THE FOOT
OF THIS TREE
SERVED AS A POST OFFICE
FOR INCOMING AND OUTGOING
WAGON TRAINS

The Hays House, dating from 1857, is near the center of the town and is the oldest or one of the oldest operating restaurants west of the Mississippi River. We shall not forget the Hays House in Council Grove, because the lady in charge was so helpful when we needed to make a telephone call to our doctor in Tucson, Arizona.

The Madonna of the Trail Monument in Council Grove is eighth in the series, and was dedicated Friday, September 7, 1928.

113

The panel on one side states:

> HERE, 'EAST MET WEST'
> WHEN THE 'OLD SANTA FE TRAIL'
> WAS ESTABLISHED AUGUST 10, 1825,
> AT A COUNCIL BETWEEN THE
> UNITED STATES COMMISSIONERS
> AND OSAGE INDIANS

The second panel:

> 1825 — 1866 TRAILSMEN
> CAMPED ON THE SPOT.
> 1847 — 1873 KAW INDIANS
> LIVED HERE.
> 1847 — FIRST WHITE SETTLER
> SETH HAYS.
> 1847 — COUNCIL GROVE
> A TRADING POST.

This Monument was rededicated September 7, 1978, fifty years after the dedication ceremony in 1928.

After spending part of the day in Council Grove, we continued west to Delavan, named for Delavan, Illinois, and founded in 1885. In a few miles we crossed the boundary into Dickinson County, created February 20, 1857, and named for Daniel S. Dickinson, who served in the U.S. Senate from New York. The town of Herington, situated just west of the boundary line, dates from 1880, when Monroe D. Herington acquired more than two sections of land in this area. He offered a right-of-way to the manager of the railroad that was being built through here, and his offer was accepted. From this start, Herington developed into a railroad center. We left Herington and our route took us west through several villages. The first one was Hope. By the 1880s, large deposits of gypsum were found in Dickinson County. This mineral is suitable for making plaster of Paris, stucco, whitewash, etc. A gypsum quarrying plant was in operation in Hope prior to 1890.

114

We continued through Elmo and Carlton, and soon after the latter, we were in Saline County. This county was named for the Saline River that flows from the western part of the state, and was established February 15, 1860. The same minerals that were produced in Dickinson County extended west into Saline County. Gypsum, our first town here, was named for one of these minerals.

Soon after 1890, several thousand tons of minerals were shipped from Gypsum to Chicago, Illinois. This raw material was used for constructing buildings for the 1893 World's Fair.

About ten miles beyond Gypsum we turned to the south, and after several miles drove through Bridgeport and into McPherson County, then soon came to Lindsborg. McPherson County was created by the state legislature on February 26, 1867, and was named for General James Birdseye McPherson. This Union general, a graduate of West Point, was killed in action on July 22, 1864, at Atlanta, Georgia.

Among the thousands of settlers who came to Kansas after it became a territory in 1854, and after statehood in 1861, there were many Swedish people who migrated here to establish homes. Some of these moved here from eastern states, but a large number came from Sweden to the United States, then settled in Kansas. On April 17, 1868, a group of these Swedish people met in Chicago, Illinois, and formed the First Swedish Agricultural Company. At some time after this date, a constitution for the company was drawn up, followed by a charter of the First Swedish Agricultural Company of McPherson County.

The Smoky Hill River has its source in eastern Colorado, then flows to the east through Kansas. At a point about halfway across the state, it veers to the southeast, and in McPherson County makes a turn to the north and enters Saline County. It was in the Smoky Valley that the Agricultural Company purchased land from the railroad. The tract of land that they bought was in the southern part of Saline County and the northern part of McPherson County.

In the fall of 1869 the town of Lindsborg was mapped out in this tract at a point about three miles south of the boundary between Saline and McPherson Counties. It was decided to name the new town Lindsborg because a number of the members of the Company

115

had names beginning with the four letters, "Lind." To these letters, "borg," the Swedish word for "city," was added, along with "s." A short time after the town was laid out, a post office was started on December 1, 1869. In this same year, a doctor opened his office in the colony on his farm near Lindsborg.

Early in 1870 a building that was large enough to be used for several purposes was erected in the village. A store was located on the ground floor, and part of the upper floor was used for community gatherings and religious services, and part of it was used for a courthouse. Within the next few years, several businesses were established including a drug store, furniture store, a harness shop, and hardware store, along with construction of a hotel.

The year 1879 was important in the history of Lindsborg, when the first railroad reached the growing community. On July 8, 1879, the city of Lindsborg was incorporated, and about three weeks later a city election was held.

Started as an academy, Bethany College in Lindsborg, by the late 1880s, had developed into an institution of higher learning with an enrollment of several hundred students.

We enjoyed our visit at Lindsborg, and while we were there, I had an opportunity to talk with two of the longtime residents of the city. They were seated on a bench in front of a Swedish shop and asked me to join them. After this, our trip continued south to the city of McPherson.

On June 14, 1873, McPherson became the county seat of McPherson County. On that date, the county seat was moved from Lindsborg, which had been the seat of government, beginning September 5, 1870. Near the courthouse in McPherson is a statue of General James B. McPherson mounted on his horse.

An event that occurred in the city of McPherson, eighteen years prior to the battle in Atlanta, Georgia, that took the life of General McPherson is commemorated by a large plaque:

THE MORMON BATTALION
at McPHERSON, KANSAS
On 3 September, 1846, the
Mormon Battalion camped near

116

here on its way to fight in the war
with Mexico.

The plaque has two columns of fifteen lines each, similar to the above. No attempt will be made here to portray the plaque in its entirety.

We drove west out of McPherson and soon we were in Conway, a town dating from the early 1880s when the railroad was built through this region. A few miles farther brought us to the town of Windom, named for William Windom. President James A. Garfield appointed William Windom as Secretary of the Treasury in 1881. In 1889, President Benjamin Harrison appointed Windom as Secretary of the Treasury in his cabinet, and he served until 1891.

About a mile beyond Windom we entered Rice County, created February 26, 1867. This county adjoining McPherson County was also named for an officer in the Union army in the Civil War, Brigadier General Samuel A. Rice. In the Battle of Salem River, in Arkansas, on April 30, 1864, General Rice was fatally wounded. He was taken to his home at Oskaloosa, Iowa, where he died July 6, 1864.

When we were about halfway through Rice County, we came to Lyons, the county seat, founded in 1876 by Truman J. Lyons. This city is situated at the center of Rice County and near the center of the state of Kansas. The Civil War monument in Lyons commemorates this tragic conflict of 1861-1865 that saved the Union.

A few miles west of Lyons at a small roadside park, a Kansas Historical Marker, "CORONADO AND QUIVIRA," is situated. This describes the entrance into Kansas of the Spanish explorer, Francisco Vasques de Coronado, in 1541. Nearby is a tall granite cross that honors Fray Juan de Padilla, the Franciscan missionary who accompanied Coronado. Fray Juan de Padilla returned to Kansas the next year and at some time after his return was killed by Indians.

Beyond the roadside park a few miles is the town of Chase, laid out more than a century ago and named for one of the officials when the railroad was built through this part of Kansas. Soon after we left

Chase, we were in Barton County, one of the counties established February 26, 1867, and named for the Civil War nurse, Clara Barton.

Clara Barton was born December 25, 1821, at Oxford, Massachusetts. Her father, Stephen Barton, had served in the army under "Mad Anthony" Wayne, then became a farmer in Massachusetts. On many of the battlefields of the Civil War, Clara Barton cared for the wounded and after the battles searched for missing soldiers.

In 1869, Clara Barton went to Europe, and while she was there became familiar with the organization known as the Red Cross, as it existed in Europe. During the 1870s, and after 1880, she worked with government officials in Washington in an effort to pass the legislation that would make the United States a member of the International Red Cross.

On June 9, 1881, although the United States had not joined the international organization, the American Red Cross was organized, and Clara Barton became its first president. At a later date, the United States joined the International Red Cross.

The following is a brief account of the achievements of this humanitarian who devoted many of her years to the saving of lives.

Clara Barton
Civil War 1861 — 1865
Franco-Prussian War 1870 — 1871
Spanish-American War 1898
Organizer and President of the
American Red Cross
1881 — 1904

Clara Barton died April 12, 1912, at Glen Echo, Maryland, at the age of ninety years.

Our first town in Barton County was Ellinwood, and several more miles brought us to the city of Great Bend, county seat of Barton County. The first settlers arrived here in 1871, and a year later the railroad reached the new settlement. By the mid-1870s Great Bend had become a busy shipping and trading point.

Except for the Mississippi, Missouri, and Rio Grande Rivers, the Arkansas is one of the longest rivers in the lower 48 states of the United States. Its source is in the Rocky Mountains of Colorado. In a general way, it flows to the southeast and enters the Mississippi River after flowing through the states of Kansas, Oklahoma, and Arkansas. In Ford County, Kansas, southeast of Dodge City, the Arkansas makes a turn to the northeast. Farther on, in Barton County, it makes the "Great Bend" where the direction of flow changes from northeast to southeast. It is here that the city of Great Bend is located. This arc-like curve of the Arkansas River was known to explorers by the year 1820 or before. Later, thousands of people who traveled over the Santa Fe Trail were familiar with this river bend.

After staying overnight at Great Bend, our first stop the next morning was at Pawnee Rock State Historic Site. Pawnee Rock was noted and described as a landmark from the earliest days of travel over the Santa Fe Trail. We found the bronze plaque that depicts William Becknell's pack train in 1821, his first trip to Santa Fe. Another plaque tells of Pawnee Rock as a camping place and lookout and is in memory of all those who traveled over the Santa Fe Trail. Near each of the plaques many names and initials have been inscribed in the face of the rock, but probably very few of these date from the days of the Santa Fe Trail. On the top of the rock a monument, "PAWNEE ROCK," stands near a stone shelter.

We left the historic site and returned to the town of Pawnee Rock, then continued on the main highway toward the southwest. Very soon we were in Pawnee County, another of the counties created February 26, 1867, and named for the Pawnee Indians. After several miles we were in the city of Larned.

On October 22, 1859, the U.S. Army established Fort Larned on the Pawnee River, west of its junction with the Arkansas River, and about thirty miles southwest of the Great Bend of the Arkansas. This military post on the frontier had the mission of protecting travelers on the Santa Fe Trail from attacks by the Indians of the Plains. The fort was named for Colonel Benjamin F. Larned of the U.S. Army. Soon after the fort was started, the first buildings of the town of Larned, named for the Fort, were put up near the junction of Pawnee River and the Arkansas. After Pawnee County was established in 1867, Larned was made the county seat and in the following years became a trading center for the region.

By 1878 the need for the fort had diminished as the danger of Indian attack decreased. In July of that year, Fort Larned was abandoned, and in 1884 the property was sold at public auction. After this it was privately owned for eighty years. In 1964 Fort Larned became part of the National Park System when it was established as a National Historic Site. A visit to the fort is an interesting experience and we enjoyed it very much.

Our visit to Fort Larned, shown above, was on a previous trip, but on this trip we stayed on the main route. Our next town was Garfield, named for James A. Garfield, the twentieth president of the United States, born November 19, 1831. Here a Wayside Chapel also honors this president.

As an infantry officer, Garfield was in several battles of the Civil War and became a major general. While still on active duty, he was elected to Congress in 1862 and was seated in the House of Representatives in December, 1863.

His political career that followed his years in the military resulted in his election as president in 1880, and he was inaugurated March 4, 1881. On July 2, 1881, President Garfield was shot by a mentally disordered gunman in Washington D.C. He died September 19, 1881, at the age of 49.

Within a few miles after we left Garfield, we entered Edwards County, created March 7, 1874, and named for William C. Edwards, a landowner in the area.

In 1873, settlers arrived from Massachusetts and established Kinsley, our next town. Named for E. W. Kinsley of Boston, this town became the county seat of Edwards County after the county was organized.

Offerle, several miles west of Kinsley, was named for a man of French descent, Laurence Offerle. He came to Kansas from Illinois, and after he surveyed the site for the town, Offerle was placed in charge of the post office.

At this small town we were pleasantly surprised to find a large mural painted on the side of a building near the highway. It was a western scene, with a cowhand driving several cattle, a tall lady with a child by her side in the center foreground, and an early-day locomotive approaching from a settlement at a distance to the right. In the background, against a bank of clouds, a shadowy caravan is crossing the prairie toward the west. The caravan consists of several men on horseback, a prairie schooner, and a number of cattle.

The author of this volume is artistically untrained, and this is my interpretation of the allegorical work of art produced by the artist. We were told while we were viewing the mural that it was the work of a local artist and, for us, it put Offerle, Kansas, on the map.

After we left Offerle we were soon in Ford County, dating from February 26, 1867, and named for Captain James H. Ford. Captain Ford was another officer in the Civil War who was honored by the state of Kansas by naming a county for him. After the war he was placed in charge of the army district that included this section of the state. We continued to the town of Spearville, named for the Boston businessman and railroad official, Alden Speare, then drove on to Wright. This village received the name of the rancher and cattleman, Robert M. Wright. Soon after we left Wright we drove into Dodge City.

In 1864, Fort Dodge, named for Colonel Henry I. Dodge, was established on the Arkansas River, where the Santa Fe Trail came close to the north bank of the river. At this place wagon trains frequently camped, and Indian war parties often raided them until the fort was built. Fort Dodge also was a supply point for troops during the campaigns against the Indians until the late 1870s.

A sod house was built in 1871 at the townsite of Dodge City, located five miles west of Fort Dodge. This was the first building in the new town; during the same year a trading post was established. In 1872 the railroad was built to Dodge City, and in July of that year plans were completed for the townsite. Soon after this, several businesses were started.

A short time after the railroad reached the new town, a post office was established. The government post office officials suggested the name Dodge City because of nearby Fort Dodge. Three years later, on November 2, 1875, Dodge City was incorporated.

For two or three years after Dodge City was founded, the buffalo trade was an important part of the business of the town. Buffalo in western Kansas numbered in the millions, and hunters brought thousands of buffalo hides into Dodge City for shipment to the east.

By late 1875, only a small number of buffalo remained in this section of Kansas. It was at this time that the cattle business began to make the wheels turn in Dodge City. Thousands of cattle were driven north over trails from Texas to the railroad at Dodge City, and these cattle drives continued for nearly a decade.

Beginning in the 1880s, many acres of grassland were plowed and crops, particularly corn and wheat, were planted. During the present century, wheat has become the leading crop in Kansas, and Dodge City is an important storage and marketing center in this section of the state. Also, many cattle are fed and prepared for market in the countryside around Dodge City and are shipped from here.

After our visit to Dodge City, we continued our trip toward the west, and we were soon in Gray County. This county was created March 5, 1887, and named for Alfred Gray, a state official who had moved to Kansas from New York in 1857. Our route followed the Arkansas River since we left Dodge City, and we were soon in Cimarron, the county seat of Gray County. From the time we left the city of McPherson, about 165 miles to the east, we were never very far from the route of the Santa Fe Trail, and it was near present-day Cimarron that the Trail parted. One fork, the Cimarron Cutoff, made a crossing of the Arkansas River and angled to the southwest. The other branch continued westerly into Colorado.

After we left Cimarron we soon drove through Ingalls, a small town named after John James Ingalls. A native of New England, Ingalls came to Kansas during territorial days and afterward served three terms in the United States Senate, from 1873 to 1891. After Ingalls, our last town in Gray County was Charleston; then we entered Finney County, established March 6, 1873.

Finney County was named in honor of David Wesley Finney, a Civil War veteran from Indiana, who came to Kansas soon after the war ended. We went through the village of Pierceville situated just west of the boundary between Gray and Finney counties. There are records that indicate that on a day in July, 1874, the inhabitants of Pierceville fled just before Indians set fire to their village. No lives were lost but the village was destroyed. We drove into Garden City, the county seat of Finney County, on Mary Street. Garden City and Dodge City are the largest cities in western Kansas.

Garden City was founded in 1878 and was known as Fulton for a few years. After the railroad was built through the area, and the population of the town increased, Garden City became the name. There are also five other population centers of various sizes in the United States that are named Garden City.

Beginning in the mid-1880s, southwestern Kansas experienced a rapid increase in population as thousands of people from the eastern and midwestern states came to the area to establish homes. Several million acres of the public domain were made available for settlement in the section of the state that extended south of Garden City to Oklahoma and west to Colorado. In a period of several years, hundreds of farm homes were built, and many of the present-day towns were established. Garden City grew rapidly during that time, and the population increased to several thousand inhabitants.

For a few years after these new farms were in operation, good crops were produced. Then a protracted drought caused much damage and many crop failures. The nationwide depression that started in 1893 brought on mortgage foreclosures, and farms were abandoned. The financial crises became very serious in western Kansas.

In 1887, construction was started on a system of irrigation ditches in Finney County and in neighboring Kearny County. Over a period of many years, the irrigated acreage in southwestern Kansas steadily increased. Alfalfa, corn, wheat, and other crops are produced on thousands of acres. Garden City is the marketing and shipping center for these crops and for the cattle that are raised in the area.

After we left Garden City, our trip continued to the west several miles, and we entered Kearny County. This county was established March 6, 1873, and named for the Civil War officer, General Philip

Kearny. General Kearny was killed during a battle in Virginia in 1862. In Kearny County we soon came to Deerfield, where we visited a park in which a stone monument honors all of those from Kearny County who served their country.

Soon after we left Deerfield our road veered to the southwest for a few miles. Then we came to Lakin, the county seat of Kearny County. This was an early station on the railroad and was named for an official of the railroad, David Long Lakin.

About a mile west of Lakin we stopped at a roadside park to see the Kansas Historical Marker, "Chouteau's Island." The island is in the Arkansas River, a few miles southwest of this park. Chouteau's Island was a landmark known from the early days of the Santa Fe Trail.

We continued west from the roadside park and soon entered Hamilton County, our westernmost county in Kansas. Almost at once we were in the small town of Kendall, and it was here that we crossed into the Mountain Time zone.

Hamilton County was created March 20, 1873, and was named for the first man who was Secretary of the Treasury of the United States, Alexander Hamilton. Soon after the Treasury Department was organized in September, 1789, President George Washington appointed Alexander Hamilton as Secretary, and he served until 1795.

We soon arrived in Syracuse, the county seat, situated near the center of the county and named for Syracuse, New York. More than a century ago there was competition between Syracuse, Kendall, and the town of Coolidge to determine the location of the county seat, and Syracuse was finally selected.

This county in the High Plains is thinly populated. In an area of nearly 1,000 square miles, there are only a few hundred people who live in the open rangeland, outside the three communities mentioned here. Coolidge is about fifteen miles west of Syracuse and is the last town on our route through Kansas. Within a mile or so we crossed the state boundary line and entered Colorado.

Chapter 10

Colorado

Our route continued to follow the Arkansas River, as it did in western Kansas, and about four miles into Colorado brought us to the town of Holly. It was named for Hiram S. Holly, a pioneer who established a large ranch in the area.

The Great Plains in eastern Colorado cover more than one-third of the state, and west of the Plains the Rocky Mountains dominate the landscape. A high plateau west of the Rockies extends to the Utah border. The highest point in Colorado is Mount Elbert at 14,433 feet. This is one of more than fifty peaks in the state that exceed 14,000 feet above sea level. It is situated in Lake County, southwest of Denver. Only one of the conterminous states of our country has a higher point; that is California, where Mount Whitney has an elevation of 14,494 feet. The Arkansas River, near Holly, is the lowest point in Colorado, with an elevation of 3,350 feet above sea level. This elevation is higher than the low point of any of the other 49 states of the United States.

When we crossed the Kansas-Colorado state boundary on our way to Holly, we entered Prowers County. Organized April 11, 1889, the county was named for a pioneer, John Wesley Prowers. When Prowers was in his early twenties he began to acquire land along the Arkansas River in Colorado Territory, and soon after this brought cattle from Missouri and turned them loose on his rangeland. In the years that followed he increased his land holdings, and they extended many miles along the Arkansas River. By this time there were thousands of cattle in his herd.

John W. Prowers was born in 1838. He lived in Missouri during his early years and arrived in Colorado before he was twenty years old. Later in life he was active in local political affairs and was in the State Legislature for a number of years. He died in 1884.

As noted previously, when the Territory of Kansas was established in 1854, the western boundary was "the east boundary of

125

the Territory of Utah, on the summit of the Rocky Mountains." Gold was discovered in 1858 within the boundary of present-day Denver, in what was then Kansas Territory.

Denver was named for James William Denver, the governor of Kansas Territory from late December, 1857, to October, 1858. In the spring of 1859, gold was found in the higher mountains west of Denver, and in other nearby areas. Reports of the discovery of gold became known, and during 1859 and 1860, thousands of men from all sections of the United States arrived in the mining camps of Colorado. Besides the mining activity in 1859 and 1860, many towns and cities were laid out, or had their start in these years. Some of these planned municipalities existed in name only and were never settled, while others developed into the Colorado towns and cities of the present time.

The Territory of Colorado was created by Congress on February 28, 1861, with William Gilpin named as the first governor. On September 9, 1861, the legislature of the new territory convened, and the creation of seventeen counties was accomplished early in the session. Many of these counties had an area larger than that of some of the eastern states of the United States. Toward the end of this first session, the legislature voted to make Colorado City the territorial capital.

When the next legislature met at Colorado City, this second session remained there only a few days, then moved to Denver to continue the legislative work. Before the session ended at Denver, Golden was selected as the capital of the territory. From 1863 through 1866, the legislature held its meetings either at Golden or Denver, and on December 9, 1867, Denver was made the permanent capital of Colorado Territory.

On March 3, 1875, Congress approved an enabling act for Colorado, a preliminary move toward statehood. The act specified that a constitution was to be drawn up. Delegates to the constitutional convention were elected, and they met in December, 1875. The constitution was framed by March 13, 1876, and the convention adjourned. A few months later, on July 1, 1876, an election was held to vote on the constitution. The vote was heavily in favor of ratification. President Ulysses S. Grant issued a proclamation on August 1, 1876, that admitted Colorado as the 38th state of the United States.

The selection of the state capital was left to a vote of the people of Colorado. By the election on November 8, 1881, Denver was chosen with a vote that was much larger than the combined total of all other locations.

Colorado, with a land area of 103,729 square miles, is eighth in size of the fifty states. The U.S. census of 1860, taken a few months prior to the date that Colorado was made a territory, showed a population of 34,277; in 1870, the population was 39,864. In 1880, four years after statehood, the census figure was 194,327, and by 1890 the population had more than doubled to 413,249. The number of inhabitants in the state increased steadily during the next century, and in 1990 the census count was 3,294,473. Denver, the state capital, had a 1990 population of 467,610.

After a brief time in Holly, we continued to the west through Prowers County, and about five miles west of Holly our highway crossed to the south side of the Arkansas River. We proceeded south of the river, and our first stop was the town of Granada. Prior to the building of the railroad in the early 1870s, the small village of Granada was situated at the mouth of Granada Creek, about three miles east of the present location of the town. The railroad company used the village as a construction railhead while the track was being laid toward the west. In 1876, Granada was moved.

We went through the village of Carlton and then soon entered Lamar, the county seat of Prowers County. Lamar was founded in 1886, and was named for Lucius Q. C. Lamar, appointed in 1885 as Secretary of the Interior by President Grover Cleveland.

The former railroad station of the Santa Fe Railroad, built in the years 1906 and 1907, is the home of the Colorado Welcome Center and the Lamar Chamber of Commerce. During our visit we were able to get a brochure that gave us the information we needed concerning Lamar and the surrounding area. Also, we were given a special edition of the newspaper published by *The Lamar Daily News*. The newspaper had photographs and historical facts concerning the role of the railroad in the history of Lamar. A headline

127

on the first page welcomed the reader to Lamar, Colorado, "The Emerald of the Plains."

The people that we met in Lamar were very knowledgeable and helpful and made us feel "at home."

Here at Lamar, we were in the section of Colorado known as the "Big Timbers." This was a growth of cottonwood trees that was nearly a mile wide and extended for many miles along the Arkansas River in the vicinity of Lamar.

For about a half century, dating from the first years of the Santa Fe Trail, caravans stopped at "Big Timbers" on their way to Santa Fe. It was the best wooded area they could find after leaving Council Grove, Kansas. Several of the exploring parties sent out by the U. S. Government during the 19th century were well acquainted with this large grove of trees.

The Indian tribes of the Plains, among them the Arapahoes, Kiowas, Comanches, and Cheyennes, used the "Big Timbers" as a camping place in order to get some protection from the storms of winter. They were doing this long before the white man came through this section of Colorado, and it was here that the mountain men carried on their fur trade with the Indians.

The Madonna of the Trail Monument in Lamar is the ninth of the series, and was dedicated Monday, September 24, 1928. It is located at the corner of South Main Street and Beech Street, a short distance from the Welcome Center.

The inscription on one panel states:

IN COMMEMORATION OF
"BIG TIMBERS" EXTENDING
EASTWARD AND WESTWARD
ALONG ARKANSAS RIVER
APPROXIMATELY TWENTY MILES
AND OF BENT'S NEW FORT,
LATER FORT WISE, 1852-1866.

On the other panel:

A PLACE OF HISTORICAL LORE
NOTED FOR INDIAN LODGES;
SHELTER FROM STORM AND HEAT;
FOOD SUPPLY FOR BEAST;
BIVOUAC FOR EXPEDITIONS;
SCENE OF MANY COUNCILS.

"THE NATIONAL OLD TRAILS ROAD" is inscribed in large letters on the back surface, as it is on other Madonna Monuments.

Our route went north over the Arkansas River as we left Lamar, then turned to the west. After a few miles we entered Bent County, named for Bent's Fort and for the Bent brothers who were early traders in the area. Pueblo County was one of the original seventeen counties created by the first territorial legislature in 1861. In 1874, when Bent County was organized, after it was taken from Pueblo County, this new county extended 105 miles, from Kansas to the eastern boundary of Pueblo County. It was 84 miles wide, from north to south. As noted previously, Prowers County was created in 1889. During that year, four other nearby counties, in addition to Prowers County, were removed from Bent County, leaving it with an area of 1,514 square miles, as it is at the present time.

Our first town here was Hasty, named for W. A. Hasty, one of the town's settlers in 1907. Several more miles brought us to Fort Lyon, a Veterans Administration medical center and site of the Fort Lyon National Cemetery. Fort Lyon was named for General Nathanial Lyon, for whom Lyon County, Kansas, also was named, as shown previously. It was at Fort Lyon that Kit Carson died.

A few miles west of Fort Lyon the highway turned to the south and went over the Arkansas River into Las Animas, the county seat of Bent County. This city and Las Animas County southwest of here were named for the Purgatoire River, discovered by early Spanish explorers. The name that they gave to this watercourse was "El Rio de las Animas Perdidas en Purgatorio."

Our visit to Bent's Old Fort National Historic Site, on a previous trip, was an interesting and worthwhile experience. The fort is

129

situated on the north side of the Arkansas River, fifteen miles west of the city of Las Animas. Bent's Old Fort was privately built and operated and was not a military post.

Charles Bent and his younger brother, William, and Ceran St. Vrain were natives of St. Louis, Missouri. They came west to the Arkansas Valley of present-day Colorado prior to 1830. In 1831, the three partners formed Bent, St. Vrain & Company, and their business was profitable over a period of more than fifteen years. Bent's Old Fort was built during 1833-1834, and was the center of operations of Bent, St. Vrain & Company.

Charles Bent, as the senior member of the firm, and Ceran St. Vrain spent little time at the Fort but took care of business operations at St. Louis, at Santa Fe, and Taos, New Mexico, and at other trading centers. It was William Bent who operated the Fort for many years. His knowledge of the Indians of various tribes, and his fair but firm dealings with them, made the Fort a successful trading post.

In the preceding section of this volume, on Kansas, a brief mention was made of John C. Fremont's explorations. On his second trip that ended July 31, 1844, his route back to Kansas was through southeastern Colorado.

> On the 1st of July we arrived at Bent's fort, about 70 miles below the mouth of the **Fontaine-qui-bouit**. As we emerged into view from the groves on the river, we were saluted with a display of the national flag, and repeated discharges from the guns of the fort,.... We were now in the region where our mountaineers were accustomed to live; and all the dangers and difficulties of the road being considered past, four of them, including Carson and Walker, remained at the fort.
>
> On the 5th we resumed our journey down the Arkansas traveling along a broad wagon-road, and encamped about 20 miles below the fort ....

After the United States Army took control of New Mexico in 1846, during the war with Mexico, Charles Bent was appointed governor of New Mexico Territory. He took office in September of that year, and during the Indian uprising a few months later, Governor Bent was killed at Taos on January 19, 1847.

The Mexican War of 1846-1848 and the warfare with the Indians that became serious in 1847, along with the death of Charles Bent, brought an end to the successful trading operations at Bent's Old Fort. William Bent closed the business, and in 1849 the Fort was destroyed by a fire. The cause of the fire is not known.

Our trip continued west from Las Animas, and in about ten miles we entered Otero County, established March 25, 1889. This county was named for Miguel Otero, born in 1829, a member of one of the leading Spanish families in New Mexico and southern Colorado. At La Junta, the county seat, we left the east-west highway we had followed from western Kansas, and traveled to the southwest toward Trinidad, about eighty miles away. At a point some miles out of La Junta, we entered the Comanche National Grassland. This is an area of several hundred square miles of range-land, with plant and animal life native to this section of Colorado. Another unit of Comanche National Grassland is situated in Colorado, southeast of here, on the boundary of northwestern Oklahoma and northeastern New Mexico.

The road to the southwest traverses a thinly populated area with very few towns. Timpas, many of whose buildings are deserted, is about fifteen miles from La Junta, and is located in the National Grassland. It was named for Timpas Creek which flows in a northerly direction and enters the Arkansas River a few miles west of La Junta. Thatcher, named for an influential pioneer, M. D. Thatcher, is south of the Grassland boundary and is about 25 miles from Timpas. We drove through Model, a dozen or so miles south of Thatcher; then a few miles farther on we exited to a state route that took us three or four miles to Hoehne. This is a larger population center, with a post office and some business places. A sign announced that Hoehne was "Home of the Fighting Farmers." This town has the name of an early settler, William Hoehne.

The Santa Fe Trail followed the Arkansas River from near Great Bend, Kansas, and at La Junta pulled away from the river and headed for Trinidad along the same route as the modern highway on which we traveled. Trinidad is situated directly on the route of the Trail and is not far from the foot of Fishers Peak, southeast of the city. This mountain rises more than 3,500 feet above the level of Trinidad and is visible from points northeast of the city. For travelers over the Santa Fe Trail, the peak directed the way to nearby Raton Pass where the wagon trains could cross the mountains.

This historic city was incorporated in 1879 and is the county seat of Las Animas County. There are many points of interest in Trinidad that relate to the Santa Fe Trail. We particularly wanted to see the equestrian statue of Kit Carson in the park that bears his name. A photograph that I took of this statue, with Gertrude standing near the base, was added to our collection of photos taken on the trip.

The last community that we visited on our trip through southeastern Colorado was Starkville, south of Trinidad. We left there and returned to the main highway, then soon crossed the state boundary into Colfax County, New Mexico.

Chapter 11

New Mexico

When a traveler crosses Raton Pass at the New Mexico-Colorado boundary, driving a modern automobile on a modern highway, it is difficult to relate to travel conditions during the days of the Santa Fe Trail. During the first forty years, prior to the 1860s, there was no road over the Pass except the rutted route made by the wagon trains. The heavy wagons were pulled from an elevation of approximately 6,000 feet at Trinidad to more than 7,800 feet at Raton Pass. Undoubtedly, this was the most difficult twenty mile stretch of the entire route.

Our trip over Raton Pass was after a moderate snowstorm, and the road was "wet and messy" (from our trip log). In a few miles we descended nearly 1,200 feet to Raton. As we continued south of the city, there was no more snow and the sun was shining brightly.

The town of Maxwell, 26 miles south of Raton, was named for Lucien B. Maxwell. About 1849, Maxwell came to New Mexico from Kaskaskia, Illinois. After we arrived in Maxwell, I went into a grocery store and asked directions to the town of French. An old map showed French at about four miles south of Maxwell, and we wanted to see the town. The man at the store advised that the town was inaccessible and that there was no way to drive there. He did not explain further, and we were led to believe that when the Interstate Highway was built through the area the town of French was either destroyed or isolated. That took care of our intended visit to French.

Volcanic action formed much of the landscape in large areas of New Mexico, and black lava beds are widely distributed. Although it is not on the route of this trip, we have visited Capulin Volcano National Monument, 32 miles east of Raton. This volcanic cinder cone rises about 1,000 feet above the surrounding countryside, and we followed the road which circles the mountain. At a viewpoint near the top we could look down into the crater.

133

Springer, with the motto, "Where the High Plains Meet the Rocky Mountain Foothills," was our next town in New Mexico. This was the county seat of Colfax County from 1882 to 1897. The county came into existence on January 25, 1869, and had two other towns as county seats prior to 1882. It was named for Schuyler Colfax who was born in New York City, New York, in 1823. Colfax was Vice-President of the United States, 1869-1873, during the first term of President Ulysses S. Grant. He died at Mankato, Minnesota, in 1885. Raton has been the county seat of Colfax County since 1897.

As we traveled south from Springer, our route for a distance was along a segment of the western edge of the Great Plains. This vast area extends several hundred miles to the east, from the Rocky Mountains that form the western boundary. After about twelve miles we entered Mora County, and here we were within sight of the rock formation, Wagon Mound. Approaching closer, this aptly named landmark lay slightly to the left of the straight highway that we were following, and the photo that I took showed that it was correctly named. The town of Wagon Mound is located at the base of this natural feature. Mora County was created February 1, 1860, and the town of Mora, situated in the western part of the county, was named the county seat.

Traveling toward the southwest from Wagon Mound, 21 miles brought us to Watrous, located at the junction of the Mora and Sapello Rivers. It was here that the Cimarron Branch of the Santa Fe Trail joined the Mountain Branch that came over Raton Pass. From the earliest days of settlement under the Spanish, the town that developed here was called La Junta, until the railroad came through in the late 1870s, at which time the name was changed to Watrous. Samuel B. Watrous came to New Mexico from New England in 1837, and by the middle of the century established a trading post at La Junta. In the years that followed he became owner of a large spread of cattle in the grazing land north of the Mora River.

The history of the settlement of New Mexico by Spain dates from the late 1590s, more than two decades before the Mayflower landed on the coast of Massachusetts. It was during the next two centuries that many present-day towns and cities had their start.

134

The year 1821 brought important changes that had far-reaching influence on the development of this future state. In that year Mexico won its independence from Spain, and it was the year the Santa Fe Trail was opened, when William Becknell made his first trip from Missouri to Santa Fe.

By the 1840s, after Texas freed itself from Mexico and was admitted as a state, in 1845, border disputes arose along the boundary between Texas and Mexico. May 13, 1846, marked the beginning of the Mexican War. On that day the United States declared war on Mexico. The next month, on June 16, General Stephen Watts Kearny led the Army of the West from Fort Leavenworth, Kansas. Their mission was to protect travel on the Santa Fe Trail, and to be prepared to invade New Mexico. Kearny followed the Mountain Branch instead of taking the shorter Cimarron Cutoff, and his army was able to reach Bent's Fort late in July. His stay there was short; he left on August 2, then pushed on to the southwest. The climb over Raton Pass was a difficult task but the army soon dropped down into the Mexican province of New Mexico.

Traveling southward, the Army of the West reached Las Vegas on August 15, 1846. This was a prosperous community of Mexican citizens, with a population of about 1,500. General Kearny read a proclamation, followed by the raising of the American flag. Three days later, on August 18, 1846, Kearny and his army took possession of the territory of New Mexico, at Santa Fe, without a battle.

For many years the grasslands around Las Vegas were used by wagon trains on the Santa Fe Trail as a camping place. Here the travelers could rest and feed their animals. On a trip of nearly 800 miles, they were now less than 100 miles from Santa Fe, but these would be difficult miles through mountainous country.

After the war with Mexico, 1846-1848, New Mexico became a Territory of the United States on September 9, 1850. The following year, in April 1851, the Secretary of War in the cabinet of President Millard Fillmore issued an order to the military commander in New Mexico to change and improve the defense system in the Territory. For many years Indian tribes had terrorized New Mexico settlements, and caravans on the Santa Fe Trail were always in danger of attack.

Following orders, the commander moved the military headquarters to the eastern section of the Territory, and in August, 1851, construction of Fort Union began. During the decade of the 1850s, Indian tribes continued their attacks, and the number of soldiers on duty in New Mexico increased regularly. Ten years after the first fort was built, an earthen fort was constructed early in the Civil War. In 1863, work was started on the third and much larger Fort Union, near the original forts. Six years, from 1863 to 1869, were needed to complete this fort, the largest in New Mexico.

For a few years after this last fort was completed, no major action against Indians took place, but in 1874 the war against the hostile tribes intensified. Much of the action occurred in the Texas Panhandle and in Oklahoma, and units from Fort Union joined in these engagements.

During the following years of comparative quiet, Fort Union continued to operate as the depot for supplying the U.S. Army in New Mexico. The arrival of the railroad at nearby Watrous in 1879 meant that change was taking place. Supply activities at the fort dwindled, and during the 1880s a small garrison was stationed here, but funds to maintain the buildings were cut off. Finally, in 1891, forty years after construction was started on the first fort, Fort Union was abandoned.

For nearly a half century after the last troops pulled out, the forces of nature took over. After a few years many of the roofs were gone, and the adobe walls began to disintegrate. Shortly before 1940, an organized local effort was begun to save the ruins that remained. After more than fifteen years, Fort Union National Monument became a part of the National Park System, on April 5, 1956. Three years later, on June 14, 1959, a visitor center and museum were opened to the public.

The road to Fort Union National Monument leaves the main highway at Watrous. This eight mile road to the Fort is parallel to the Mountain Branch of the Santa Fe Trail for most of the distance. We enjoyed our visit to this historic fort, and we found it very interesting.

The boundary between Mora County and San Miguel County is crossed soon after leaving Watrous. The Territorial Legislature set up San Miguel County on January 9, 1852. Continuing to the southwest through this county, we soon came to Las Vegas, the county seat. The early history of Las Vegas, during the days of the Santa Fe Trail, was mentioned here previously.

This city is sometimes referred to as "the other Vegas." It is without many of the bright lights and much of the glitter of its namesake farther west. More than three decades after the Mexican War of the 1840s, the railroad reached Las Vegas in 1879. People from the eastern and midwestern states and a number of immigrants from Europe settled here, and Las Vegas experienced a period of prosperity. Many homes were built, and by the earliest years of the present century Las Vegas was the largest town in the territory.

It was the building of so many homes, some dating from the Mexican period prior to the American take-over, and many more built during the century that followed, that has left Las Vegas with a diverse architectural background. Approximately 850 buildings in the city have been placed on the National Register of Historic Places.

An incident that occurred during our earlier travels will be mentioned here. Nearly every year we planned a summer vacation trip, and over a period of several years we were able to see many points of interest in the eastern states.

It was in the mid-1960s that we went beyond the Mississippi River, on a trip to Arizona. On this trip I had a lesson in mountain driving, even though the mountains were not the highest mountains in the west.

The timing of our trip brought us to Dodge City, Kansas, about the middle of the May, and we stayed here overnight. The next morning we started early, heading southwest, and crossed the Oklahoma Panhandle and a corner of the Texas Panhandle. Early in the afternoon we stopped briefly in Tucumcari, New Mexico. At Dodge City, I had called ahead for a reservation at a motel in Las Vegas, New Mexico. The map showed Conchas Lake State Park on what appeared to be a fairly direct route to Las Vegas. Since we had plenty of time, we decided to go that way instead of via the Interstate Highway and U.S. route.

We arrived at the state park, did some bird-watching, then prepared our evening meal, and took our time while we ate it. While G was taking care of the dishes, I decided to reload the car before leaving. The May sun seemed to be descending slowly in the western sky and finally, early in the evening, we started on the 75-mile trip to Las Vegas, via the state route that showed as a narrow black line on the map.

Within a little while the sun dipped behind the hills and mountains, and soon after that, a couple of flatlanders from northern Ohio were traveling over a strange mountain road in the dark. It was at about this time that I realized that I had gone through Tucumcari without buying gasoline, and now the gauge was heading toward empty. I did not want to alarm G, so I said nothing, and glanced at the gasoline gauge only about once each minute. We remembered afterward that we met a total of five vehicles on the trip from the state park to the vicinity of Las Vegas.

When we reached a high point on the highway and I saw the lights of Las Vegas below us, I began to breathe freely again. At the first filling station we came to, I filled the tank with gasoline, and finally told G how I had worried on the trip. She knew all the time what was going on and had read me completely.

After our visit to Las Vegas on the present trip we moved on, and in about ten miles came to Tecolote. The history of this village had its origin in 1824 when the first settler arrived, only three years after Mexico gained its independence from Spain.

After leaving Tecolote, we followed the Interstate Highway nearly thirty miles and exited at the road that took us to the town of Rowe, then on to the Pecos National Historical Park, situated two miles south of the town of Pecos. The inscription on the Official Scenic Historic Marker relates the history of the early development and later decline of the Pecos Pueblo.

In 1541, Pecos Pueblo stood 4-5 stories high and accommodated a population of 2,000. The Spanish built two mission churches here in the seventeenth and eighteenth centuries. Disease, famine, economic hardship, drought, and Comanche raids all took their toll. In 1838, 17 inhabitants of Pecos moved to Jemez Pueblo where their descendants live today.

In 1965 the ruins of the pueblo became Pecos National Monument, administered by the National Park Service. Twenty-five years later, in 1990, the name was changed and it became Pecos National Historical Park. The designation on the historic marker was still for the monument, as shown above, when we visited here on our trip.

Soon after we left the historical park we entered Santa Fe County, named for the city of that name. Santa Fe was made the county seat when the Territorial Legislature created the county on January 9, 1852. The village of Gloricta is in Santa Fe County, a short distance west of the county boundary. It was at Glorieta Pass that a Civil War battle was fought.

The battlefield is marked by another Official Scenic Historic Marker:

GLORIETA BATTLEFIELD
The decisive battle of the Civil
War in New Mexico was fought
at the summit of Glorieta Pass
on March 28, 1862. Union troops
won the battle when a party of
Colorado volunteers burned the
Confederate supply wagons, thus
destroying Southern hopes for
taking over New Mexico.

After visiting the Glorieta Battlefield we continued to Santa Fe. In traveling from the town of Rowe to Santa Fe we had encircled the southern end of the Rocky Mountains of North America. The mountains south of here in the state are isolated peaks or small ranges and are not generally considered as part of the Rockies.

On January 6, 1912, New Mexico entered the Union as the 47th state. The Capitol building, dedicated in 1966, differs from the other capitol buildings of the United States in that it is circular and has four entrances. The official emblem of New Mexico is the Zia sun symbol, and the design of the Capitol building follows this theme. A guided tour of the building gave us an opportunity to go into the House chamber. When we reached the office of the governor we saw the portraits of the early Spanish governors of New Mexico, and those who have held the office during the Mexican and American eras.

Canyon Road, with its retail stores, restaurants, and galleries, was of interest to us, and in this area there are a number of well-preserved historic houses. We were able to go into the beautiful Cristo Rey Church with its altar screen of hand-carved stone.

The Plaza has been located at the center of Santa Fe since the provincial capital was established by the Spanish governor in 1609-1610. Historical records indicate that the Palace of the Governors, located on the north side of the Plaza, was built during the latter year. This is now a museum with exhibits that depict New Mexico history since the earliest days.

Our visit to the Mission of San Miguel of Santa Fe, located a few blocks from the Plaza, was an interesting experience. One of the postcards that we purchased in the city states that this is the oldest church in the United States, built in 1610. The very thick adobe walls and the supporting beams above the nave, including the massive beam that supports the choir loft, have stood the test of centuries.

The bell on display in a nearby room is of historical interest. The casting, poured in Spain in 1356, weighs more than 700 pounds and is made of copper, silver, iron, and gold. The bell was used in Spain and then brought to Mexico. Early in the nineteenth century it was moved from Mexico to Santa Fe by the primitive transportation available at the time and placed here in the tower of the Mission. In the decade of the 1950s, the bell was brought down from the tower and moved to its present location.

The Cathedral of St. Francis of Assisi is about a block east of the Plaza. Archbishop Jean Baptiste Lamy arrived in Santa Fe soon after 1850, and in 1869 the cornerstone of the Cathedral was laid. After his death, the Archbishop was buried under the altar of the Cathedral.

Also situated near the Plaza, southwest of the Cathedral, is the Loretto Chapel, dedicated in 1878. Since that time, its spiral staircase, built by an unknown carpenter under mysterious circumstances, had made this chapel a widely-known attraction in this capital of New Mexico.

Santa Fe has many more points of interest in addition to those mentioned above. There are several museums and dozens of art galleries and shops. A few blocks south of the Plaza stands a house that is thought to be the oldest in Santa Fe. Here I photographed a sign that goes a step beyond this, "Welcome to the Oldest House in the U.S.A."

The Santa Fe National Cemetery is situated less than two miles north of the Plaza. Soldiers killed in the Indian wars are buried here, and also those who lost their lives in the Civil War battles that were fought in New Mexico.

Leaving Santa Fe we traveled to the southwest, going from an elevation of 7,000 feet above sea level to an elevation that would be 5,000 feet when we arrived at Albuquerque. We soon crossed the county boundary into Sandoval County, established by the Territorial Legislature on March 10, 1903. A few years ago when we were in this area, we stopped at the large, well-known Santo Domingo Indian Trading Post on the Santo Domingo Indian Reservation and purchased a signed pottery bowl and some turquoise jewelry. Then we went into beautiful Santo Domingo Mission Church, with its painted symbols of Indian ponies adorning the exterior of the church.

Algodones, about a dozen miles south of Santo Domingo Pueblo, is a town near the Rio Grande River that was settled in 1839. Several miles farther south brought us to Bernalillo, the county seat of Sandoval County. The Coronado State Monument, established March 7, 1935, is across the Rio Grande River, two miles northwest of Bernalillo.

As we continue south, we are traveling down the valley of the Rio Grande River which flows through New Mexico to the Mexican border. The river then continues to the southeast from El Paso, Texas, and forms the boundary between Mexico and the United

141

States from this point to the Gulf of Mexico, near Brownsville, Texas.

Soon after we left the city of Bernalillo, we entered Bernalillo County, set up by the legislature of New Mexico Territory on January 9, 1852. Continuing southward, as we were approaching Albuquerque, we went through Alameda, where an Indian pueblo was located until about 1700.

Bernalillo County is one of the smallest counties in the state in land area, but its population is the largest of any county in New Mexico. Albuquerque, the county seat, is the largest city in the state; the 1990 census figure for the city was 384,619.

Points of interest that we had visited in Albuquerque on past trips include the following:

Old Town. The first settlers of Albuquerque arrived here in 1706. Situated around Old Town Plaza are arts and crafts shops, galleries, and restaurants. The San Felipe de Neri Church, at a corner of the Plaza, dates from the same year that the earliest settlers arrived in the area.

Indian Pueblo Cultural Center. This is a museum with shops where authentic Indian crafts and art works are sold. Included are pottery, sand painting, weaving, jewelry, etc., produced by the Pueblo Indians of New Mexico.

University of New Mexico. The Art Museum here has changing exhibits, and we were pleased to see works of Georgia O'Keeffe when we were there. At a Plaza on the campus of the University, the ship's bell from the USS New Mexico is displayed.

Sandia Peak Aerial Tramway. The lower terminal of this tramway is a few miles north of Albuquerque. We made this 2.7 mile tramway trip which goes to the upper tram terminal on Sandia Peak. The Four Seasons Visitor Center of the Cibola National Forest is located in this upper terminal. The round trip ride in the tram above the rugged terrain of the Sandia Mountains is a memorable experience.

Following our plan on the present trip, we stayed overnight, then the next morning went to McClellan Park where the Madonna of the Trail Monument, number ten, is located. Our early October visit was during the annual Albuquerque International

142

Balloon Fiesta, so we had an opportunity to see many of the colorful balloons in the air.

The dedication and unveiling of this Madonna Monument took place on Thursday, September 27, 1928. The inscription on one face of the monument is as follows:

INTO THE PRIMITIVE WEST
FACE UPSWUNG TOWARD THE SUN,
BRAVELY SHE CAME,
HER CHILDREN BESIDE HER.
HERE SHE MADE A HOME,
BEAUTIFUL PIONEER MOTHER!

The other inscription reads:

TO THE PIONEER MOTHER OF AMERICA
THROUGH WHOSE COURAGE AND SACRIFICE
THE DESERT HAS BLOSSOMED.
THE CAMP BECAME A HOME,
THE BLAZED TRAIL THE THOROUGHFARE.

On the fiftieth anniversary of the unveiling of the Monument in Albuquerque, a rededication program was held on September 27, 1978 at McClellan Park.

The snapshots I took of the Madonna of the Trail Monument, in the early morning light and shadows, would not win a prize but they are adequate. We soon left the park and drove south out of Albuquerque. Our first stop was at the Isleta Pueblo with its mission church facing the large plaza.

Leaving Isleta, we entered Valencia County, established by the Territorial Legislature on January 9, 1852. This was the date on which several counties in New Mexico were created. We soon came to Bosque Farms, then a few more miles south brought us to Peralta. The county seat of Valencia County, Los Lunas, is situated just west of the Rio Grande River, and we soon crossed over the river and arrived there. Continuing our route to the south, in about ten miles we reached Belen.

Several miles beyond this town, we entered Socorro County. This county, while still under Mexican rule, had been established in 1844. In July, 1850, before New Mexico officially became a territory of the United States, the Territorial Legislature made this a county. Of the 33 counties in New Mexico, four have a land area of more than 6,000 square miles, and Socorro County is one of these four counties.

Along the Rio Grande River in New Mexico there are a number of small towns and villages on both sides of the river. Many of these appear on highway maps, but some are omitted, and these are also omitted from this book. When we reached Bernardo, about sixteen miles south of Belen, we crossed to the east side of the Rio Grande, then turned to the south and continued to the town of La Joya. In the 1700s this Spanish settlement was the gathering place for caravans traveling down the Camino Real to present-day El Paso, Texas. After a brief stop here, we returned to Bernardo.

Continuing our journey to the south, we went over the Puerco River which enters the Rio Grande just north of La Joya. This river has its source in northern New Mexico, nearly 150 miles north of its junction with the Rio Grande River. In a few miles we came to San Acacia. Before we reached Socorro, we visited the towns of Polvadera and Lemitar, the latter about seven miles north of Socorro. San Acacia, Polvadera, and Lemitar are west of the Rio Grande River and east of the Interstate highway, which parallels the river.

The city of Socorro is the county seat of Socorro County, and its history goes back to the early days of Spanish settlement, prior to 1600. San Miguel Mission, completed in 1821, was built on the site of an earlier mission that was built in 1627. We had been in Socorro a number of times, and visited the church with its beautiful paintings and handcarved pews and interior beams.

Silver was discovered in the mountains west of Socorro in the late 1860s, and during the decade from 1880 to 1890 silver and lead were mined in large quantities. Wagon trains and later the railroad transported the ore to smelters in Socorro. The city grew rapidly, and for a few years it was the largest city in New Mexico Territory. Socorro is the home of the New Mexico Institute of Mining and Technology, founded more than a century ago.

144

We took the U.S. highway west from Socorro to Magdalena. Here an Official Scenic Historic Marker told of the mining activity in the surrounding mountains.

MAGDALENA

Magdalena is located in a mineral-rich area which became a center of silver mining in the 1860s. In 1885, a railroad was built to the smelter in Socorro, and Magdalena became an important railhead for cattle, sheep, and ore.

Moving onto the west, in 25 miles we came to the entrance road that leads to the National Radio Astronomy Observatory — Very Large Array. This is situated on the Plains of San Agustin at an elevation of 7,000 feet above sea level.

The Very Large Array (VLA) is the world's largest radio telescope and consists of 27 antennas each of which is 82 feet in diameter and weighs 210 tons. The antennas are portable and are moved by a special 92 ton transporter which runs on railroad tracks arranged in the shape of a V. They can be positioned on any of 72 stations along the railroad tracks to meet the scientific objectives of the observations in progress.

The VLA is the most sensitive telescope in the world for making detailed radio pictures of objects throughout the Universe.

The information noted above was presented on a large sign near the highway, along with several lines of additional scientific data.

The Very Large Array was constructed during the 1970s, and the last telescope was finished in 1979. On October 10, 1981, the completed VLA was dedicated.

We drove to the Visitor Center which is situated nearly four miles from the main highway. Here we took the self-guided tour of the exhibits and saw the slide show.

After our visit at the Observatory we continued our trip, and soon entered Catron County, with the largest area of any county in

145

New Mexico. It is sparsely populated, with only a few towns and small villages. One of these is Reserve, the county seat, located toward the southwestern corner of the county. This county was established on February 25, 1921, when the State Legislature separated this large area from the western part of Socorro County. It received the last name of Thomas Benton Catron, born in 1840, who was selected in 1912 by the legislature as one of the U.S. Senators to represent the new state of New Mexico.

Our next town was Datil near the northwestern edge of the Plains of San Agustin. From here the highway enters the mountains west of Datil and soon goes through a section of the Cibola National Forest.

From the Canadian border of the United States to the border with Mexico, the Continental Divide follows a zigzag course across the western United States. Here in New Mexico, the highway we are following crossed the Divide at an elevation of 7,796 feet at a point nearly twenty miles northwest of Datil. Two miles west of this summit brought us to Pie Town, and in that distance the elevation above sea level dropped nearly 1,000 feet, to just over 6,800 feet. Perhaps we were there at the wrong time of the day, or at the wrong time of the week, but there was no discernible activity at Pie Town. I have a photograph of Candelaria's TRADING POST, Pie Town, New Mexico, taken that day, but the sign in red letters on the door said "CLOSED."

Our highway map of New Mexico shows the village of Omega, fifteen miles west of Pie Town, but when we arrived there we saw a sign, "Omega," but did not see a village. In less than ten miles from this sign we came to Quemado, our last town in New Mexico. After Quemado we drove about 32 miles through open grazing land with few habitations, then crossed the New Mexico-Arizona state line into Apache County, Arizona. We continued through sparsely settled terrain and reached Springerville, about 16 miles west of the boundary line.

From Albuquerque, in addition to the route through Socorro that we traveled on this trip, there is a more direct route to Arizona. A few months before our trip through Socorro, and west to Springerville, we traveled via this route so we could visit the

Indian towns and the pueblo of the Laguna Indian Reservation. This alternate route is described in the following paragraphs.

The Interstate Highway goes in a westerly direction after leaving Albuquerque, crosses the Bernalillo-Cibola county boundary, then traverses the Laguna Indian Reservation. Continuing westward to Grants, then to Gallup, this main highway enters Arizona some 22 miles west of Gallup.

About fifteen miles after the Interstate enters Cibola County, a state highway is reached from an exit, north to the Indian town of Mesita. This state route runs roughly parallel to the Interstate for many miles, in a westerly direction, north of the main highway. There are a number of small towns or villages that are situated along this state route, and these can also be reached by exits from the Interstate.

Following the state highway to the west from Mesita, in a few miles the traveler comes to the Laguna Pueblo. There are nearly twenty pueblos in New Mexico, and Laguna is well-known, partly because of its location near a much traveled highway. From a parking area on the Interstate there is a fine view of this pueblo.

The small Indian village of Paraje is a few miles west of Laguna, and a sign above the trading post indicates that this is the home of THE PARAJE TRADING COMPANY. Settlements are close together here, and the Indian village of Casa Blanca is a short distance beyond Paraje. Cubero, just west of the Reservation boundary, is only two miles or so beyond Casa Blanca. San Fidel, first settled in the late 1860s, is the next town after Cubero, and the U.S. post office at San Fidel has the Zip code, 87049. When we were there, the Stars and Stripes were flying from a high flagpole near a corner of the building.

For the traveler through this section of New Mexico, going either east or west, Mount Taylor is a prominent feature of the landscape. The mountain, with an altitude of 11,301 feet, is north of the Interstate, and is almost directly north of the town of San Fidel. The rest areas on the highway, in the vicinity of MP 103, are excellent places from which to view this mountain that is snow-capped many months of the year.

About a mile west of the rest areas just mentioned, a highway sign on the Interstate reads: Exit 102 — ACOMA — SKY CITY. On a previous trip that we made to this section of New Mexico, we visited Acoma Pueblo, located on the Acoma Indian Reservation, about thirteen miles south of the Interstate Highway. The following is a brief description of the Sky City, and what we saw on our guided tour.

We drove to the visitor center located near the base of the mesa, and paid for the tour, then had time to go into the museum. The price included the bus trip up the steep road to the top of the mesa, which is 357 feet above the surrounding countryside, also the tour of the Pueblo, and the return trip by bus.

The young lady who was our guide for the walking tour of Acoma was very knowledgeable, and the descriptive account shown below is based on the facts that she gave during the tour.

The Pueblo covers seventy acres and the homes are owned by residents of the Acoma Indian Reservation. Many of the people who own the homes live in the communities of Acomita and McCartys, and in the adjacent area north of Acoma. Some own homes at the Pueblo and live in them during weekends. Our guide told us that the permanent population of Acoma was about forty people.

An interesting part of the tour was our visit to the San Esteban del Rey Mission which was established in 1629. It is massively built with thick walls and heavy ceiling timbers. The mission is more remarkable when it is considered that everything used in building it was brought to the top of the mesa either by burros or on the backs of men.

As we continued the walking tour we passed or stopped at a number of pottery stands in front of the homes. At one of these we purchased a small signed pot. The tour ended at the headquarters, and we soon rode the bus down to the visitor center. In a short time we were on our way from Acoma after an enjoyable visit to the Sky City.

We returned from Acoma Pueblo to the main highway by the same route we followed in the morning, then drove to McCartys.

This is a community named for the contractor who had his headquarters here during the days of railroad construction.

At a point several miles west of the Indian Reservation road that goes south to Acoma, a state highway exits from the Interstate and goes in a southerly direction. It is the route to El Malpais National Monument, established in the late 1980s to set aside and preserve many square miles of the lava beds that are south of Grants, New Mexico. This route also leads to the vicinity of the large natural arch, La Ventana, about twenty miles south of Grants.

Some eight miles west of the highway to El Malpais National Monument, another state highway leaves the Interstate and heads toward the south from a point near the city of Grants. After passing through the village of San Rafael, this road continues south, then veers to the west and crosses the Continental Divide. Forty-three miles from its starting point near Grants, this highway reaches El Morro National Monument, located in the Ramah Navajo Indian Reservation.

This National Monument was established in 1906, during the Administration of President Theodore Roosevelt. From the visitor center, a walk of a few hundred feet takes the visitor to the petroglyphs at the base of the Inscription Rock. The oldest of these, carved by Spanish explorers more than 390 years ago, are quite clear and legible. Americans carved their names here, beginning in about the year 1850. One long name has the date 1859 inscribed below. It is very precise and exact and shows remarkable carving skill.

Prior to our present trip, we had visited El Morro National Monument on two occasions. On one of these trips I made plans beforehand to hike to the top of the mesa. My interest in doing this came from reading about the Lorenzo Sitgreaves expedition of 1851. Its mission was to explore and map this area of New Mexico, and on west through present-day northern Arizona. Doctor Samuel Washington Woodhouse was physician and naturalist of the expedition, and his discovery of the White-throated Swift (*Aeronautes saxatalis*) added this species to the list of North American Birds.

"This beautiful Swift I saw whilst encamped at Inscription Rock, New Mexico. Being on top of this high rock at the time without my gun, I was unable to procure specimens. I had a fair view of the birds at this time, as they flew close to me. I descended immediately and procured my gun; but the birds by this time flew too high for me to be able to procure a shot at them. They were breeding in the crevices of the rocks."

After viewing the petroglyphs we returned to the visitor center so I could get information concerning the trail. It was a day in August and the sky had become overcast. The ranger on duty explained the route I should take, then gave me this advice, "If it becomes stormy and there is thunder or lightning, come down at once." Having hiked for years in the mountains of Arizona, I knew that he was right. I went to the top, explored the rock formations and took some photographs, then came down. I was in no danger, but one of my snapshots showed that the clouds had darkened and it was time to leave.

The road to the west after leaving El Morro National Monument enters the Zuni Indian Reservation. Here a colorful entrance sign states, "YOU are Entering ZUNI-LAND — Welcome." This state route that had its beginning near Grants goes across the Zuni Reservation. It passes through several small communities before reaching Zuni, site of the Zuni Pueblo. A roadside sign — ZUNI — Village Limit — Elev. 6280. SPEED LIMIT 30 — is at the entrance. About fourteen miles west of Zuni the road crosses the New Mexico-Arizona state line.

The Interstate Highway that goes from Albuquerque west to Arizona passes through the northern tip of the extensive lava beds that are south of Grants. At a point about halfway between the exits to the El Malpais and El Morro National Monuments, a state highway leaves the Interstate toward the north and goes through the city of Grants. This highway then continues toward the northwest, parallel to the main highway, for a distance of approximately twenty miles.

Grants, the county seat of Cibola County, was first settled in 1872 and became an important station on the railroad after the tracks reached the village in 1881. The town of Milan is a few miles to the northwest of Grants. At a point several miles beyond Milan, a highway sign announces, "Welcome to Bluewater Village."

150

Both the Interstate and the state highway enter McKinley County a few miles to the north of Bluewater. Named for William McKinley, 25th President of the United States, McKinley County was established February 23, 1899, and Gallup became the county seat in 1901. The village of Prewitt is situated on the state highway about four miles north of the county boundary. After passing through Prewitt, the state highway ends when it joins the Interstate. The through highway continues to the west and in ten miles reaches the town of Thoreau.

A few years ago our travels took us to northern New Mexico for several days and we were at Farmington. Our plans were to go south and visit Chaco Culture National Historical Park, which could only be reached by traveling over dirt roads. The directions that I received at Farmington were not correct, as we found after wandering around a while over miles of dusty roads. Finally, we stopped at a small store and a lady gave us directions that were correct, and we made it to the Park.

Our available time allowed us to visit some of the ruins, and the film presentation at the visitor center explained the history of the Anasazi culture. A Park Ranger suggested that our best route from the Park would be to go south. After twenty miles of dirt road, we would reach the pavement that would take us to the Interstate highway. We followed his directions and arrived at Thoreau without further delay.

Five miles west of Thoreau the Interstate highway crosses the Continental Divide, and near the exit there are several small business places. Continuing on, the highway goes through the northern portion of the Fort Wingate Military Reservation and in a few miles reaches Gallup.

This city had its beginning in 1881, the year the railroad was built through this part of New Mexico, and it was named for a railroad official. Located as it is, just east and south of the Navajo Indian Reservation, and north of the Zuni Indian Reservation, Gallup is an important trading center.

As mentioned previously, the direct route from Albuquerque, via the Interstate Highway, enters Arizona west of Gallup.

Chapter 12

Arizona

After our trip across western New Mexico and into Arizona, by way of Socorro, we spent part of the day in Springerville. The first settlers arrived here in 1871, and four years later Harry Springer opened a store. His business lasted less than a year, and he left the area, but his name has remained since that time. A few years after his departure the residents decided that the town should be called Springerville.

When the First Territorial Legislature of Arizona organized the new territory on November 8, 1864, it consisted of four large counties. These were Yuma, Mohave, Pima, and Yavapai. Nearly fifteen years later, the legislature established Apache County, on February 24, 1879, by separating it from Yavapai County. In that year, Saint Johns became the county seat, but in 1880 Springerville was made the seat of county government. In 1882 county records were returned to Saint Johns, and it has been the county seat since that year.

The Madonna of the Trail Monument in Arizona is located on the main street of Springerville. It was dedicated Saturday, September 29, 1928, two days after the dedication of the Monument in Albuquerque, New Mexico.

The inscription on one side states:

CORONADO
PASSED HERE IN 1540
— HE CAME TO SEEK GOLD —
BUT FOUND FAME

On the other side of the Monument the inscription reads:

A TRIBUTE TO THE PIONEERS
OF ARIZONA AND THE SOUTHWEST

WHO TROD THIS GROUND
AND BRAVED THE DANGERS
OF THE APACHE
AND OTHER WARRIOR TRIBES.

As was noted earlier, Spain was involved in the exploration and settlement of New Mexico until 1821, when Mexico won its independence. After that year, Mexican forces were stationed there for more than a quarter century until after the war between the United States and Mexico in the 1840s. Spanish troops and later Mexican troops were also present in Arizona during that period, but in smaller numbers, and mostly in the southeastern portion of the present-day state. The principal garrison was at Tucson.

In October, 1846, two months after General Kearny captured Santa Fe without a battle, the Mormon Battalion, commanded by Lt. Col. Philip St. George Cooke, marched out of Santa Fe. The Battalion went south through New Mexico, then turned toward the west. After many delays and slow going, Tucson was reached by mid-December. They met little resistance and on December 17, 1846, the American flag was raised over the town.

The Treaty of Guadalupe-Hidalgo between the two countries was signed February 2, 1848. This treaty ceded a large area to the United States, including Arizona north of the Gila River.

Arizona became a territory on February 24, 1863, when it was separated from New Mexico, and Prescott was made the capital. In 1867 Tucson became the capital of Arizona Territory and remained the seat of government for a decade. Despite strong opposition from the residents of southern Arizona, the capital was moved back to Prescott in 1877.

The city of Phoenix in central Arizona had its start in the late 1860s when a small company was formed to grow crops in the irrigated Salt River Valley. Within two or three years a town was laid out and lots were sold. The new town was situated in the southern part of Yavapai County and the territorial legislature established a new county on February 12, 1871, that included this area. This was Maricopa County; Phoenix became the county seat after an election in May, 1871.

154

The growth of population in Phoenix and the Salt River Valley was slow during the early years of the 1870s, partly because 1873 was a depression year throughout the nation. During the last years of the decade, business conditions improved and there was an increase in the population. By 1880 Phoenix was approaching 2,000 inhabitants.

A proposal to incorporate the growing community resulted in the signing of a petition by many residents, and the request was approved by the legislature. In early 1881 a charter bill was signed by the territorial governor, and this allowed the town of Phoenix to incorporate. Early in May, in the first election after incorporation, the voters elected a mayor and other officials.

The acreage devoted to agriculture in the Salt River Valley increased after June, 1885, when a new canal began to bring more water to the valley for irrigation. As more agricultural products were produced, it became necessary to develop new markets. Early in 1881, the second transcontinental railroad in the United States was completed, when tracks laid from California across Arizona were joined in New Mexico to tracks laid from the east. In July, 1887, a railroad built from Phoenix joined this main line at Maricopa, south of Phoenix, thus linking the Salt River Valley with the outside world.

Early in 1889 the capital of Arizona Territory was permanently moved from Prescott to Phoenix. The population of the Salt River Valley increased steadily during the decade of the 1880s, and in 1890 Phoenix had more than 3,000 inhabitants.

The population of Arizona Territory in 1870 (the first census of the territory) was 9,658; it increased to 40,440, in 1880; in 1890, it reached 88,243. During the 1890s and after the turn of the century, delegations were sent to Washington, D.C., to ask Congress to make Arizona a state. A constitutional convention was authorized, and in December, 1910, a constitution was enacted.

The population growth of Arizona Territory had continued, and the census of 1910 was 204,354. The people of the territory were strongly in favor of statehood, and after meeting the requirement for a constitution, the remaining obstacles that blocked admission as a state were finally removed in 1911 and early in 1912. On February

14, 1912, by Presidential proclamation, Arizona became the 48th state of the United States.

The population of Arizona continued to grow steadily after statehood, and in 1940 the census figure was 499,261. A half-century later, in 1990, the number of inhabitants had increased to 3,665,339, and population growth was continuing.

After our visit at Springerville we drove north past Lyman Lake and made a brief stop at Lyman Lake State Park. In an enclosure here there are several buffalo that can be readily seen or photographed. Continuing northward, we were soon in Saint Johns.

Stewart L. Udall and his brother, Morris K. Udall, prominent Arizona political figures, were born in Saint Johns and spent their early years there. Stewart was elected as a representative to Congress from Arizona in the 1950s. After President John F. Kennedy took office, Stewart Udall was appointed to the Cabinet as Secretary of the Interior, a position he held under President Kennedy and President Lyndon B. Johnson. Morris Udall entered the House of Representatives in 1961 and was reelected to consecutive terms until failing health forced his retirement. In 1976, Morris ran for President, but Jimmy (James Earl) Carter became the nominee and was elected to a four-year term.

The U.S. highway from Saint Johns to Holbrook goes west five miles out of Saint Johns, then turns toward the northwest. From this point, a state route continues west eleven miles to the village of Concho, originally settled prior to 1870. In this small village there are a number of old, abandoned adobe houses. It is probable that these were built when the early settlers arrived there.

From Concho, a state highway took us north to the route from Saint Johns to Holbrook. We followed this main highway toward the northwest, and soon crossed the Little Colorado River. In about a dozen miles we reached the boundary between Apache County and Navajo County. The latter county was created on March 21, 1895, when it was separated from Apache County.

Soon after we entered Navajo County, we came to the southern entrance of Petrified Forest National Park. In 1906, during the presidency of Theodore Roosevelt, this area became the Petrified Forest National Monument, and in 1962 it was made a National

156

Park. We have visited this park at other times, and on this present trip we did not include it in our itinerary. After passing the entrance road to the National Park, we proceeded to Holbrook, the county seat of Navajo County.

The railroad was built through this area in 1881, and Holbrook had its start the next year. The new town was named for an official of the railroad. In 1887, only five years after Holbrook was first settled, a deadly gunfight occurred in the small town.

The sheriff of Apache County had a warrant for the arrest of a man charged with stealing livestock. On September 4 or September 6, 1887 (accounts differ as to the date), he was in Holbrook to make the arrest of the suspect. The sequence of the events that followed is unclear, but when the officer went to the door of the house where the suspect was staying, shooting started within seconds. The sheriff's first shot mortally wounded the man he came to arrest; then he continued firing. In quick succession, he killed the suspect's teenage brother, who was armed and ready to fire at him; then wounded a resident of the house who fired one shot in his direction, and, when a family relative hurriedly left the house, the sheriff killed him instantly. The place where this shooting took place more than a century ago is well marked, and I took a photograph of the residence.

Previously in this book, in the New Mexico segment, the direct route from Albuquerque to the Arizona boundary through Grants and Gallup was described. The following paragraphs briefly described the Arizona portion of this route to Holbrook, via the Interstate highway.

Lupton, named for a railroad official in the early years of the 1900s, is the first community in Arizona. Nine miles west of Lupton is Houck, with its Fort Courage Trading Post. The Trading Post consists of a grocery store and gift shop, and there is a U.S. post office.

Continuing westerly, after several miles the Interstate highway reaches the small town of Sanders, then comes to Chambers. This settlement started as a trading post in the 1880s, and when the railroad was built through northern Arizona, the station was named for the owner of the post.

157

After this main highway enters Arizona, it cuts diagonally across the southeastern tip of the Navajo Indian Reservation for a distance of nearly twenty miles. This is the largest Indian Reservation in the United States. It occupies the northeastern part of Arizona and extends across the state boundaries into Utah and New Mexico. The Hopi Indian Reservation, most of which is in Navajo County, Arizona, is situated in the western portion of the large Navajo Reservation and is completely surrounded by the latter.

The only place in the United States where four states meet is designated as the Four Corners, located in the northeastern part of the Navajo Indian Reservation. Here Colorado, Utah, Arizona, and New Mexico join, and it is the site of the Four Corners Monument.

Continuing to the west from Chambers, mentioned previously, the small community of Navajo is located near the south side of the Interstate highway, six miles beyond Chambers. After leaving Navajo and proceeding sixteen miles farther west, the Interstate arrives at the northern entrance to Petrified Forest National Park. The Painted Desert Visitor Center is near the entrance, and this is also the Park Headquarters. This direct route from Albuquerque to Holbrook reaches the latter city about 25 miles west of the National Park.

We were in Holbrook part of the afternoon, then continued west toward Winslow. At some point along here, a road sign advertised "Sparkling Restrooms," and two or three miles or so farther on another sign stated "Clean Restrooms." We noticed the difference, and Gertrude wrote in the log, "They deteriorated fast."

Winslow became an important shipping point in 1881 after the railroad reached the town. It continues as an important trading center for a large surrounding area. Like many other towns and cities that have resulted from railroad construction, Winslow received the name of a railroad official.

Soon after we left Winslow we entered Coconino County, and nineteen miles west of the county boundary, a road leads to Meteor Crater, located six miles south of the Interstate highway. Various estimates have been made concerning the time in the distant past when a meteorite struck the earth at this place. These estimates range from more than 20,000 years ago to almost 50,000 years

158

ago. The dimensions of the meteorite are unknown, but its weight has been estimated as thousands of tons, and its diameter as more than eighty feet. The approximate measurements of the crater are 4,100 feet across at the rim and 570 feet deep.

An attempt was made early in the present century to drill down to the meteorite. At a depth of just over a quarter of a mile, the drill struck an object that it could not penetrate, and the work was stopped.

A visitor center and museum acquaint the visitor with the history of Meteor Crater, and there is a display of meteorite fragments. On the outside, visitors have access to observation decks built over the crater.

After returning to the main highway from Meteor Crater, and proceeding three miles to the west, the ruins of Two Guns are in sight. The photo that I took shows the remains of several buildings, some without roofs and others with only parts of walls standing. The site covers quite an area, and I do not know whether any of the structures were inhabited.

Near Two Guns the highway crossed Canyon Diablo. In December, 1853, Lieutenant Amiel Weeks Whipple, in command of the survey for a railroad near the 35th parallel of north latitude, named this canyon. Unable to get his survey party across this steep-walled chasm, he went north along the eastern edge, more than twenty miles, before he could cross and proceed westward.

Continuing west toward Flagstaff, we stopped briefly at the town of Winona, situated to the north of the highway. After a few more miles we came to the road that goes south three miles to Walnut Canyon National Monument. In a deep gorge here, cliff dwellings were built and inhabited by Sinagua Indians eight centuries ago. A steep paved trail leads to a number of these dwellings, and many can be seen from the rim of the canyon. The monument was established November 30, 1915, and covers more than three square miles. At the visitor center, information can be obtained about the strenuous round trip hike into the canyon.

It is about seven miles from the National Monument entrance road to Flagstaff, the largest city in northern Arizona. Coconino County was established February 19, 1891, and Flagstaff was made the county seat during the same year. On June 4, 1894, the town was incorporated. This city is the home of Northern Arizona University, the Lowell Observatory, and the Museum of Northern Arizona. Situated in the high plateau country of northern Arizona, Flagstaff is near the San Francisco Peaks. Humphreys Peak in these mountains, at 12,633 feet, is the highest point in Arizona.

Going west out of Flagstaff, we soon came to Bellemont, a vestige of a town with a few aged buildings. Seven more miles brought us to Parks, whose store has a sign, "Parks in the Pines." After traveling west of Parks a distance of twelve miles, we came to Williams.

Situated at the foot of Bill Williams Mountain, and named after the nineteenth century mountain man, Bill Williams, the town came naturally by its name. Williams was first settled in 1876, and after the railroad was built through here in 1882, the town became an important shipping point for lumber and cattle. Over the years it has become an active tourist center with facilities for the traveler.

This is a good place in this volume to go forward a few months and tell of a trip from Tucson to this part of Arizona early in the next summer. As part of this trip, we planned to drive up Bill Williams Mountain; we also wanted to ride the train to the Grand Canyon.

Soon after we arrived in town, we drove to the Ranger Station. Here we were told that the road up the mountain was suitable for a passenger car. Early in the afternoon, we took the paved road out of Williams toward the mountain. After about five miles, we turned to the right on a gravel road that was marked with a sign, "Seven miles to the top." For more than six miles the road was well-graded, "except for a few sharp turns where it was rough and rocky." "The last half mile was pretty rough but we kept going". (The quotations are from our daily trip log that Gertrude wrote.)

When we arrived at a place near the top where I could turn the car around, I did so. G. stayed in the car while I hiked the short distance to the lookout. There I had a brief conversation with two men who said they were servicing equipment in use here on the top of Bill Williams Mountain. I took a few photos near the lookout, then returned to the car. We drove slowly down the mountain and returned to Williams.

160

Before our trip up the mountain, we had purchased tickets for the train trip to the Grand Canyon which we would take the next day. Regular rail passenger service to the south rim of the Canyon started in 1901 and continued until 1969, when it was discontinued. In September, 1989, the Grand Canyon Railway began round trip excursion runs from Williams to Grand Canyon Village in Grand Canyon National Park.

Early in 1989, rebuilding was started on the entire rail system. This involved the replacement of thousands of railroad ties and the laying of many miles of track, along with the repairing of bridges and station facilities. Railroad coaches and steam locomotives were acquired and completely restored before they were put into service.

The rail trip of more than 63 miles from Williams to the south rim of the Canyon traverses a varying landscape. This includes forests of pinyon pine, ponderosa pine, and juniper, and miles of open range. Shortly after leaving Williams, the route is through the southern unit of the Kaibab National Forest for a distance of about three miles. As the train proceeds north, after several more miles there is an opportunity to see the higher north rim of the Grand Canyon in the distance. Soon after this, the towering San Francisco Peaks can be seen in the east. About nineteen miles south of the Grand Canyon the tracks enter the northern unit of the Kaibab National Forest. Travel is through this forest until the National Park is entered at a point that is nearly four miles from the south rim.

The stopover at Grand Canyon Village allows enough time to enjoy a lunch and to visit some of the many shops. From the paved rim trail the visitor can view the vast Grand Canyon of the Colorado River.

The return trip to Williams offers vistas of changing colors, as the sun slowly goes down in the western sky. We enjoyed our round trip by railway from Williams to Grand Canyon National Park. It was a day that we would remember.

As mentioned some pages back, it was during the 1960s that we visited Arizona for the first time. On that trip we drove to the Grand Canyon, and we visited there many times since then.

Months before leaving Ohio on this first trip to the Grand Canyon State, we wrote for reservations to make the muleback trip down into the Canyon from the south rim. We had decided to visit Oak Creek Canyon prior to going to the Grand Canyon, and this was a good decision.

We made the trip south from Flagstaff, via the highway that traverses the Coconino Plateau. This road drops steeply into Oak Creek Canyon from the plateau, and, needless to say, I drove with extreme caution as we proceeded downgrade over this unfamiliar route.

The cabin we had reserved for a stay of one night in the canyon worked out well. It gave us time to see the colorful cliffs, rock formations, and other natural features of this scenic canyon. Also, we had an opportunity to visit the city of Sedona. Here there are galleries and many shops with pottery, jewelry, sculptures, and painting.

We left Oak Creek Canyon and went back through Flagstaff to Grand Canyon National Park, where we had reservations for two nights at Yavapai Lodge. The next morning we were at the meeting place near the head of Bright Angel Trail, where ten hardy souls, five men and five women, were ready for the muleback trip. The cowboy who was in charge of our group told us the basic facts we needed to know in order to have a safe ride down into the canyon.

Our leader then selected a mule for each member of the group. My wife, at five feet and a fraction of an inch tall, drew a small mule and was near the head of the group of riders. Since my height approaches six feet, I was placed on the largest animal and was given the last place in line. I know that I am an inexperienced horseman, and that big mule also knew it. Telling me to control him would have been a waste of time. That mule did just what he wanted to do on the whole trip, but it brought me back safely.

With the cowboy at the head of the train, the mules, surefooted at all times, moved down the Bright Angel Trail at a steady pace. After I became accustomed to the ride on the narrow trail, beside the deep canyon, I felt more at ease, knowing that similar trips have been made for many years. Stops were made where water was available for mules and humans, and at these places the riders could dismount. Talking with Gertrude at one of the early halts, I found that she was doing all right and was enjoying the experience.

162

Ours was the one-day trip down into the canyon, and we would return to the rim by late afternoon or early evening. When we reached Indian Gardens, a shaded area where water is available, we stopped briefly, then took the trail across the plateau to Plateau Point. Here we could see and photograph the Colorado River, nearly one-fourth mile below. We returned to Indian Gardens, where the mules were fed and given time to rest. The riders had time to relax and eat the lunch that had been prepared for us at Grand Canyon Village and carried down from the rim.

After our midday break we began the slow climb out of the canyon. This is hard work for the mules, especially on summer days when it can become very hot in the canyon. Rest stops and water stops are essential, both for the mules and for their riders, and the cowboy in charge kept his eyes open to see that no problems developed on the way to the rim. Finally, we finished the climb and, one by one, a tired group of muleback riders reached the starting place of the day's trip.

Although this trip down into the Grand Canyon occurred some years ago, this method of seeing and experiencing the canyon has changed very little over the years. In the 1990s, groups of people on mules see the Grand Canyon just as they have for many decades. Restrictions still are in effect concerning the minimum height of those who ride the mules, as well as the maximum weight that is allowed.

Resuming the account of our coast-to-coast trip, we left Williams after staying briefly, then proceeded to the west. In about twenty miles, we came to the town of Ash Fork, where the entrance sign announced, "WELCOME to ASH FORK — FLAGSTONE CAPITAL of USA." A few miles west of here, the Interstate Highway sets a new course, leaving the "Old Highway" that was the route of travel across northern Arizona for many years.

Some road signs designate this "Old Route 66" as "Historic Route 66," and it is shown on highway maps as Arizona "State Route 66." This was part of "Route 66," the federal highway from Chicago to Los Angeles beginning in the 1920s.

It was at Williams, east of Ash Fork, that the last official U.S. signs designating "Route 66" were removed in 1985, after this highway ceased as a certified federal highway.

Our next town was Seligman, where the entrance sign shows an elevation of 5,250 and states that the town was founded in 1886. At this town the Interstate highway is still fairly close to "Old 66," but west of Seligman "66" heads to the northwest, and the Interstate continues westward toward Kingman.

State Route 66 traverses a valley for several miles and about 25 miles to the northwest enters the Hualapai Indian Reservation. Two miles or so before the highway reaches the reservation boundary there is a turnoff to Grand Canyon Caverns.

The State Route turns from its northwest direction and goes toward the west as it enters the Hualapai Indian Reservation. The highway soon enters Mohave County, then bends toward the southwest in the direction of Peach Springs, where the Hualapai Indians have their tribal headquarters. A circular inscription on a building near the highway advises that this is the Hualapai Tribal Forestry Department, Peach Springs, Arizona. After covering a distance of nearly twenty miles across the southern end of the Indian Reservation, State Route 66 goes through Truxton, nine miles southwest of Peach Springs, and a couple of miles beyond the reservation boundary. We continued to the southwest, and in ten miles arrived at Valentine, named in honor of Robert G. Valentine, Commissioner of Indian Affairs early in the 1900s. Five miles beyond Valentine, we came to Hackberry, then followed State Route 66 to Kingman, a distance of nearly thirty miles.

The city of Kingman, county seat of Mohave County, dates from its start in 1883 as a station on the railroad that was built across northern Arizona. It was named for Lewis Kingman, an official of the railroad. When the territorial government of Arizona was organized in 1864, Mohave County was established on November 8 of that year. The county seat was moved to Kingman in 1887 and has remained there since that time. Kingman was incorporated January 21, 1952, after an election resulted in a vote that was strongly in favor of incorporation.

State Route 66 continues southwest of Kingman, and after a few miles the road ceases as a state route. It is shown on the highway map as Historic Route 66. We followed this old highway through the Black Mountains. The roadway was rough in places and, by driving with care, it was passable and safe.

After several miles, the Historic Route climbs and goes over Sitgreaves Pass, then soon reaches the ghost town of Goldroad. This abandoned town has gone the way of most such towns after the ore is depleted. The rock walls of a few buildings still stand, but many of the buildings were adobe, and these are becoming mounds of earth.

Continuing beyond Goldroad, the old highway comes to Oatman after two or three miles. Oatman had its start soon after 1900, when gold was discovered nearby. Successive discoveries of gold in the area kept the town active as a mining center for about thirty years. A number of the buildings date from the early days of Oatman, and some of these are in use as retail shops.

In the course of our present ocean-to-ocean trip we were morning visitors in Oatman, and did not see any of the wild burros that often are seen by tourists who visit the town. On a previous trip to western Arizona, we saw several burros on the main street in the center of Oatman.

Leaving Oatman and traveling toward the south, we came to the community of Golden Shores after about twenty miles. The Fort Mohave Indian Reservation extends along the Colorado River, to the west and southwest of Oatman. We passed a sign at a road intersection: "Fort Mohave Indian Reservation Agriculture Area."

Beyond Golden Shores, in a few more miles we came to Topock. This town is reached by the Interstate Highway, which makes a turn to the south near Kingman, then goes west and crosses the Colorado River at Topock.

Our trip through Arizona ended at Topock, when we drove across the bridge above the Colorado River and entered California.

Chapter 13

California

The history of California since the arrival of the first Europeans dates from the first half of the sixteenth century. On September 28, 1542, Juan Rodriquez Cabrillo entered San Diego Bay and gave it the name, San Miguel. A few months after this, another Spanish sea captain sailed farther north and reached Cape Mendocino on February 26, 1543, then turned back to the south. More than three decades later, on June 15, 1579, the English explorer, Francis Drake, sailed into the bay in Marin County, presently known as Drake's Bay. Drake claimed the land for England and named it New Albion.

After the turn of the century, Sebastian Vizcaino, on November 10, 1602, took his ship into the bay that Cabrillo had named San Miguel. Vizcaino changed the name to San Diego de Alcala. Leaving the bay, Sebastian Vizcaino sailed on toward the north, where he changed the names of several places. Among those he renamed are Santa Barbara, Point Conception, Monterey Bay, and Point Reyes.

Mission Basilica San Diego de Alcala was founded by the Franciscan friar, Father Junipero Serra, on July 16, 1769. This was the first of 21 missions established in California. Mission San Gabriel Arcangel, in the city of San Gabriel, was founded September 8, 1771.

In 1774, Juan Bautista de Anza traveled overland from Sonora, in northern Mexico, to the mission at San Gabriel. The next year, on August 16, 1775, the Spanish authorities named Monterey as the capital of California. In March, 1776, on his second overland trip from Sonora, Anza decided where the presideo at San Francisco should be located, and on September 17, 1776, the presideo was dedicated.

Another of the missions founded by Father Junipero Serra was San Juan Capistrano on November 1, 1776. This mission is well-known for the return of the swallows from Argentina each year at the same time in March.

September 4, 1781, was the date that the city of Los Angeles had its beginning, when several families founded a pueblo here under the leadership of a Spanish official.

The first American ship to tie up at a port in California came from Boston and docked at Monterey, October 19, 1796. In 1812, Spanish authorities in California could not prevent Russians from establishing Fort Ross on the coast north of San Francisco. Several years later the fort was closed and the Russian forces withdrew to the north. In 1814, a sailor from an English ship became the first person of foreign descent to reside in California, and on January 15, 1816, the first American settled there.

Mexico became independent from Spain in 1821, and on November 19, 1823, the Mexican Republic was established. California was officially made a territory of the Mexican Republic on March 26, 1825; ten years later, on May 23, 1835, Los Angeles became the capital of California territory. The capital was returned to Monterey in August, 1838. The first overland wagon train reached California from Missouri on November 4, 1841. Manuel Micheltorena took over as governor of California on December 31, 1842. He was the last governor appointed by Mexico.

In May, 1846, the Mexican War started when the United States declared war, as stated here in the New Mexico segment. On July 7, 1846, the American Pacific fleet took over Monterey. The next month, on August 13, Los Angeles was taken by American forces under the command of the military governor of California. For several days in early December, 1846, the Battle of San Pasqual was fought near present-day Escondido, California. The last battle of the Mexican War in California took place on January 9, 1847, at La Mesa.

The decisive battles of the Mexican War were fought in Mexico after United States troops landed near the city of Vera Cruz on March 9, 1847. Several battles were fought as the American troops pushed toward Mexico City, and in September, 1847, the capital of Mexico was taken by the United States forces. On February 2, 1848, the Treaty of Guadalupe Hidalgo was signed and the United States acquired California and New Mexico. By the terms of the treaty, the United States paid Mexico $15,000,000. Reference to this treaty was made in the Arizona segment.

The discovery of gold in 1848 and the gold rush that soon started brought rapid change to California. Early statehood was a consequence of the increase in population that resulted from the rush to the gold camps. Many thousands of men came from all sections of the United States and from other countries. On April 4, 1850, Los Angeles was incorporated as a city, and on September 9, 1850, California entered the Union as the 31st state. Sacramento became the state capital on February 25, 1854.

Before the Congress of the United States voted to admit California as a state, the first 27 counties were created by the California legislature on February 18, 1850. The population of the new state increased rapidly during the decade of the 1850s, and in 1860 the census was 379,994. Steady growth continued, and by 1900 the population of California had increased to 1,485,053.

It was in 1900 that irrigation of the Imperial Valley in southeastern California began, when canals first carried water from the Colorado River to this section of the state.

The preceding paragraphs are intended as a partial outline of the early history of California. During the twentieth century, which is now in its final years, the population of this state has become by far the largest of any state of the Union, with a 1990 census of 29,758,213.

No attempt will be made in this volume to write a complete history of California since the beginning of this century.

We arrived in the city of Needles after traveling sixteen miles toward the north on the California side of the Colorado River. Named for a group of needle-like pinnacles several miles to the southeast on the Arizona side of the river, Needles was founded in 1883 when the railroad arrived at the Colorado River.

The Old Trails Monument, situated on Broadway near Palm Way, is a memorial of a Mojave Indian trail that was used by early explorers who came through this area.

When we crossed the Colorado River and entered California south of Needles, we were in San Bernardino County. The area of this county is 20,062 square miles, the largest of any county in the

United States. It has a larger area than that of each of the nine smallest states in the country. Another measure of its size is that the area of San Bernardino County is several thousand square miles larger than the combined areas of the four smallest states. The county was created April 26, 1853.

After staying overnight in Needles, we continued our trip toward the west the next morning. We were now in the Mojave Desert, and would travel more than 145 miles before leaving it. Elevation above sea level of this desert varies from less than 1,800 feet to nearly 5,000 feet, with a few peaks of the scattered mountain ranges above 6,000 feet. Dry desert lakes form part of the floor of this plateau, along with numerous parched valleys.

The first town we visited west of Needles was Goffs, located several miles north of the Interstate highway. This town was founded as a station on the railroad when it was built through this part of California in 1883. Several of the towns and villages in the Mojave Desert that were established when the railroad came through have the same names as towns that are farther east in the United States.

The road that brought us to Goffs from the east turned toward the southwest at this town. After crossing the Interstate, this road continued a few miles to a junction with the Old National Trail Highway near the village of Essex. Next to the STOP sign at the intersection, a rectangular sign with an arrow pointing west stated AMBOY 34 Mi. A small inset below the arrow indicated that this was Route 66, designated in California as HISTORIC ROUTE 66.

A road sign at Essex showed a population of 100 and the elevation 1,775. From Essex, a road to the northwest goes across the Interstate highway and continues to the Providence Mountains State Recreation Area, site of the Mitchell Caverns Natural Preserve.

The tiny hamlet of Danby, about ten miles southwest of Essex, is situated on the railroad just south of the Old National Trail. It is marked by a railroad sign, "DANBY," standing near the tracks.

After leaving Danby, we continued on the Old National Trail Highway to the village of Chambless. Here a metal plaque, dated May 3, 1992, was located across the street from a market. This told the history of Route 66.

OLD ROUTE 66
PERHAPS NO OTHER HIGHWAY IN THE U.S. IS AS FABLED
AS OLD ROUTE 66. IT HAS BEEN IMMORTALIZED IN SONG,
LITERATURE, AND EVEN A T.V. SERIES AS THE MAIN
STREET OF AMERICA. AUTOMOBILES CAME EARLY TO
THE DESERT, FOLLOWING THE RAILROAD WITH ITS RE-
LIABLE WATER SOURCES. IN THE EARLY 1900S THE
ROUTE WAS KNOWN AS THE NATIONAL OLD TRAILS
ROAD. IN 1926 IT BECAME U.S. HIGHWAY 66, AND WITHIN
A DECADE WAS PAVED ALL THE WAY FROM L.A. TO CHI-
CAGO. HEAVY TRAVEL BY DUST BOWL EMIGRANTS LED
JOHN STEINBECK TO LABEL IT THE MOTHER ROAD.
CHAMBLESS, WHERE YOU NOW STAND, WAS A TYPICAL
ROADSIDE STOP. IT WAS BYPASSED BY INTERSTATE 40
IN 1973, AND THE ROUTE 66 DESIGNATION WAS OFFI-
CIALLY DROPPED IN 1985.

BILLY HOLCOMB CHAPTER
THE ANCIENT AND HONORABLE ORDER
E. CLAMPUS VITUS
MAY 3, 1992

After our visit at Chambless, we drove toward the west and
soon came to Amboy, thirteen miles beyond Chambless. The Amboy
Crater, a gray-black volcanic cinder cone, is located not far to the
west of Amboy. In the photograph that I took from across the flat
desert, it resembles a small, 200-foot high mesa. Traveling on to
the northwest, lava hills and other remains of lava flows can be
seen from the Old National Trail Highway as it continues toward
Ludlow. After leaving Needles, we were never far from the railroad line that was built through here more than a century ago, and
we saw eastbound and westbound freight trains.

At Ludlow the Old National Trail Highway rejoins the Interstate highway. According to our road map, we had traveled 61 miles
to the west on this road that runs roughly parallel to the high-speed
main route. This town was named for William B. Ludlow when the
railroad was built through this area. Going on to the west from

Ludlow, after about seventeen miles we passed to the north of the Pisgah Crater. A lava flow extends to the Southeast for several miles from this crater.

We moved on to the small town of Newberry Springs. For a few years early in this century, the name of this town was changed to Water, because the springs here furnished the railroad with an ample water supply. Later the original name was restored.

Our next town was Daggett, only a few miles east of Barstow. The history of Daggett dates from its founding in the 1860s, but it was the discovery of silver in the nearby Calico Mountains that was instrumental in the development of the town. By 1882, silver ore was being processed at a stamp mill here, and in that year the railroad was built from Mojave to Daggett.

Originally called Calico Junction, the railroad officials changed the name to Daggett, for John Daggett who was lieutenant governor of California during the years 1883 to 1887. Previously, this government official had mapped out the Daggett townsite and was one of the first to build a house here.

Silver mining in the Calico Mountains became unprofitable after several years and ended in the mid-1890s. Before this, borax mining started in these mountains and by 1902 the output of three borax mines brought prosperity to Daggett. The town had stores, restaurants, a lumber yard, and a hotel in 1902, the peak year for borax production.

We were soon in Barstow, a city in the Mojave Desert, or High Desert, of southern California. It is an important railroad city at the junction of two Interstate highways.

One of these Interstates originates at the Canada-Montana border and goes in a southerly direction across Montana, Idaho, and Utah. In southern Utah it veers toward the southwest, then goes across the extreme northwest corner of Arizona. Continuing to the southwest, the highway crosses the southern tip of Nevada and enters California. After about 100 miles it reaches Barstow.

The other Interstate highway begins in North Carolina, near the Atlantic Ocean, and proceeds westerly to Tennessee. After going to the west across that state, the highway goes over the Mississippi River at Memphis, then continues toward the west across

172

Arkansas and Oklahoma. It then goes through the Texas Panhandle and continues through New Mexico and Arizona to the Colorado River. The river is crossed into California, south of Needles, and the Interstate goes westerly from Needles, about 145 miles to Barstow.

Travelers arriving in Barstow via either of the Interstates have alternate routes from this city that will take them to points in California. The north to south Interstate highway that reaches Barstow from Nevada heads on toward the southwest and goes over Cajon Pass, then continues south to San Diego. It gives access to the large population of southern California.

In addition to the Interstate highway that goes south of Barstow, a major state highway goes to the west through Mojave and Tehachapi to Bakersfield. From here the highway system makes coastal points, as well as central and northern California, available for travel.

From Barstow another state route can be taken that goes toward the southeast, mostly through open country. This highway can be used to reach Joshua Tree National Monument and other areas in the southeastern section of the state.

In 1886, a railroad line built from the south through Cajon Pass joined the transcontinental line at Barstow. The town was named Waterman Junction, but early in 1886 the name was changed to Barstow. This was the middle name of William Barstow Strong, the president of the transcontinental railroad.

The city of Barstow is located near the Calico Mountains, at an elevation of 2,106 feet above sea level. Barstow College, a two-year community college, was founded in 1959, and its enrollment has increased over the years. In the center of the city, the Harvey House commemorates the era of railroad passenger transportation. This historic landmark is one of the establishments built to serve meals to passengers who were traveling by railroad in the late 1800s and in the early years of the present century.

Calico Ghost Town is situated ten miles northeast of Barstow in the Calico Mountains. This San Bernardino County Regional Park is a restored 1880s mining town.

After our overnight stay at Barstow, we continued our trip, going toward the south via the north-south Interstate highway. Our next stop was at Victorville, situated in the Victor Valley, about 32 miles south of Barstow and twenty miles north of Cajon Pass.

By the 1820s, Jedediah Smith and other explorers brought expeditions through Victor Valley and over Cajon Pass on their way south. Although strongly resisted by the Indians of the area, a number of Mormons from Utah settled on ranches in the Valley prior to 1870.

More settlers arrived in Victor Valley after the railroad was constructed from National City, near San Diego, north through the Cajon Pass and to Barstow. In 1885, the telegraph station in the Valley was named Victor, for Jacob Nash Victor, a construction official of the railroad. Later this became the name of the community that was served by the railroad. When the post office was established here in 1901, postal officials changed the name to Victorville to avoid confusion with the town of Victor, located near Colorado Springs, Colorado.

Victorville is situated a short distance north of the San Bernardino Mountains, at the south edge of the Mojave Desert. Population growth was slow until a few years after World War II, then increased during the next four decades. On September 21, 1962, Victorville was incorporated as a city. Victor Valley College was founded here in 1961, and its enrollment has increased to several thousand students. There are also a number of trade schools in this city, whose population was 40,674 in 1990.

The California Route 66 Museum in Victorville opened to the public on November 11, 1995. It commemorates and tells the story of Route 66. In 1926 this became the "Main Street of America," extending from Chicago to Los Angeles.

Leaving Victorville, we followed the Interstate to the south, then left the highway at the exit to Hesperia and drove into that city. Hesperia is on the Mojave River, in the central part of Victor Valley.

During the 1850s, the first building was put up in Hesperia. It contained a small store, a stable, and there was space for several bunk beds. It was nearly thirty years after this that a dependable water supply became available in this community. In early 1886, a legal action went into effect that allowed water to be diverted from the Mojave River for use in Hesperia.

Three ranches for raising grapes were started, and these furnished employment for many people. The grapes from the ranches were important in the development of the raisin industry of Southern California. Besides grapes for raisins and for wine, other fruits were grown here.

By the late 1880s, Hesperia started to grow and, as the population increased, several buildings were constructed. In 1890 a modern brick hotel was completed, and by the turn of the century many travelers from the east stopped at Hesperia. As the automobile became more popular for cross-country travel, Hesperia was important as a place to stop for parts and repair services before the trip over steep Cajon Pass. In 1924 this situation changed when the new transcontinental highway was built through Victorville and bypassed Hesperia.

In the 1950s, three decades after this highway change, an important real estate transaction took place. This involved the purchase of thousands of acres of land in the Hesperia area. Within a few years after the mid-1950s, many businesses were started. The population increased rapidly during the following years. The city of Hesperia was incorporated in 1988. In 1990 the census showed a population of 50,418.

After our visit to Hesperia, we returned to the Interstate highway and continued toward the south over Cajon Pass. The highway goes downgrade for several miles, from an elevation of more than 4,200 feet at the Pass to less than 1,100 feet at San Bernardino. We passed through the community of Devore and soon arrived at San Bernardino.

The city of San Bernardino had its start with the arrival of nearly 500 Mormons from Salt Lake City in 1851. Early in 1852 they purchased land in San Bernardino Valley, and soon after that the town of San Bernardino was laid out. Two years later, on April 13, 1854, the city was incorporated and was made the county seat of San Bernardino County. In the century that followed, the city developed with the coming of the railroad and later the advent of automobile travel.

The population of the city of San Bernardino made a strong increase during the decades after World War II. The census count of 1990 for San Bernardino was 164,164 inhabitants.

This city is the home of two institutions of higher learning that each have an enrollment of several thousand undergraduates:

San Bernardino Valley College is a two-year college, founded in 1926.

California State University, San Bernardino, is a four-year university, founded in 1965.

We visited the San Bernardino Library during our stay in the city. Most of our time was spent in the California Room, and we found this interesting and informative concerning the history of California. The two ladies there were well-informed and were helpful to us.

After spending the night at San Bernardino, we continued our trip toward the west following Foothill Boulevard, which is also Historic Route 66. Records indicate that in 1853 the Mormons cleared a road through the heavy brushland west of their settlement of San Bernardino. As more people settled in the area during the years that followed, this road was improved and was extended on to the west. Eventually, as Foothill Boulevard, it became part of the transcontinental highway from Chicago and points east to Los Angeles.

We were soon in the city of Rialto, four miles west of San Bernardino. During the two decades prior to 1880, a few settlers established homes in this area. In the 1880s, after the railroad came to this part of California, many people arrived in this section of the state.

Rialto had its start in 1887-1888 when several families from Kansas settled here. Water was available, and citrus crops could be grown successfully. Before long these families were joined by other settlers, and in the twenty years from 1890 to 1910, the population of the town gradually increased.

The community had grown to 1,500 residents by 1911, and incorporation was being discussed. Petitions were signed to put the question on the ballot. On October 31, 1911, the vote was in favor of incorporation, and Rialto became an incorporated city.

From the earliest days of settlement, citrus groves were planted and for years citrus furnished employment for many people of Rialto. The peak years for citrus production were the 1930s. During that decade there were nearly 4,000 acres of oranges and grapefruit in Rialto. By the end of World War II the acreage of citrus had declined substantially, and this trend continued. In 1965 there were about 100 acres of oranges in the Rialto area.

Thirty-nine years after incorporation, the census figure for Rialto in 1950 was 3,156. This was only a little more than twice the count of 1,500 in 1911. The growth of the city increased rapidly beginning in 1953, and in 1960 the population was 18,000.

A new Civic Center was dedicated on October 31, 1961, when Rialto celebrated its fiftieth anniversary as an incorporated city.

Rialto continued to grow during the 1960s, 1970s, and 1980s, and the census of 1990 showed a population of 72,395 inhabitants.

After our visit to Rialto we drove into Fontana as we continued westward. This city had its beginning in 1906 with the purchase of 18,000 acres in the San Bernardino Valley by Mr. A. B. Miller. A new town named Rosena was started on this land, and the name was changed to Fontana in 1913. After railroad lines were established through the new city, several factories were built there prior to 1930.

In the early 1940s, during World War II, the Kaiser Steel Mill was built in Fontana by Mr. Henry J. Kaiser. It was the availability of dependable rail transportation that was an important factor in the selection of Fontana for the new steel mill. On time delivery of the materials needed for steelmaking and shipment of steel to customers were essential requirements.

The growth of the city continued after the second World War, and Fontana was incorporated on June 25, 1952. During the years that followed the population increased greatly, and in 1990 it was 87,535.

Continuing to the west from Fontana, via Foothill Boulevard, we soon reached Rancho Cucamonga. This city is situated near the foot of the San Gabriel Mountains and is almost directly south of Cucamonga Peak, a mountain in the southeastern part of the range. Within the next thirty miles the route that we were following would take us to several cities that are located near the base of these mountains.

As was noted here earlier, the first settlers in Victor Valley, north of Cajon Pass, met resistance by the Indians of the area but were able to establish ranches there.

For several centuries before the first Spanish explorer, Juan Bautista de Anza, arrived in the Cucamonga Rancho region, Indians were living here. It was these Indians who gave the valley its name, Cucamonga. This tribe was not warlike and allowed the area to be settled peacefully.

The year 1839 marked the beginning of the modern history of Rancho Cucamonga. In that year the area where the city had its start was part of 13,000 acres of land granted to a Mexican citizen by the Mexican government. Named the Cucamonga Rancho by the citizen who received the grant, the land had been used for sheep and cattle grazing prior to 1839. Under the new owner it became an important area for the production of grapes, and this resulted in the establishment of the oldest wine-making plant in California. This winery is still in operation here.

In 1858 the Cucamonga Rancho changed hands, and the next year the acreage of grapes was enlarged by the new owner, John Rains. Two years later, in 1860, this landowner built the first house in California that used fire-burned brick in its construction. Known as Casa de Rancho Cucamonga, the "Rains House" is a registered national historical landmark.

In 1864, during the presidency of Abraham Lincoln, the first post office was established in Rancho Cucamonga.

During more than a century after this, the city continued to grow, and it became an incorporated city as the result of an election held on November 8, 1977.

In the decade of the 1980s, the population of Rancho Cucamonga increased very rapidly, and in 1990 the census count was 101,409.

We left Rancho Cucamonga, and Upland was our next stop. It was here that we would see the Madonna of the Trail Monument, number twelve, the Monument farthest west.

178

Soon after it was settled, the area that is now the city of Upland became important in the production and marketing of agricultural products. Many acres of citrus fruit and grapes were grown, and these provided much of the income for the residents of Upland. After the railroad was built through the town, these crops could be shipped to population centers in the East.

On May 15, 1906, Upland was incorporated. During the next decades the population increased, and it became a residential community. Retail businesses were established as business activity expanded. After World War II the growth of the city accelerated during the years that followed. In 1990 Upland had a census count of 63,374 inhabitants.

We proceeded to the Madonna of the Trail Monument at Foothill Boulevard and North Euclid Avenue. This Monument was dedicated February 1, 1929, and in February, 1979, a rededication ceremony was held.

One inscription states:

THIS TRAIL, TROD BY
THE PADRES IN SPANISH
DAYS, BECAME
UNDER MEXICAN RULE,
THE ROAD CONNECTING
SAN BERNARDINO AND
LOS ANGELES, LATER
THE AMERICAN POST ROAD.

The other inscription is as follows:

OVER THIS TRAIL
NOVEMBER 1826,
JEDEDIAH SMITH, SEEKING
A RIVER FLOWING WESTWARD,
LED A BAND OF SIXTEEN
TRAPPERS, THE FIRST
AMERICANS TO ENTER
CALIFORNIA OVERLAND

179

This completed our goal of seeing all of the Madonna of the Trail Monuments, but our trip would continue westward to the Pacific coast.

A few miles west of Upland brought us to Claremont. The first settler arrived here in 1871, and the community was able to grow slowly during the years that followed. In 1887 the railroad reached Claremont, and soon after this a railroad depot and a hotel were built, along with a few houses.

In 1888 the first orange trees were planted in the Claremont area. Within a few years after this, the growing and marketing of oranges became an important industry and furnished the income for many people of Claremont. Citrus crops increased to more than 3,000 acres during the first decades of the twentieth century, but the acreage declined after the Second World War.

In 1907 Claremont was incorporated. The city is well-known as the home of the Claremont Colleges, incorporated on October 14, 1925. This is a group of six colleges and several institutions that are affiliated with them.

On an earlier trip through Southern California we visited the Rancho Santa Ana Botanic Garden, located on North College Avenue. This is one of the institutions affiliated with the Claremont Colleges. It can be visited daily at any time during the years, except for a few holidays.

Like many other California cities, the population of Claremont increased rapidly after World War II. In 1990 the census was 32,610.

Still following Foothill Boulevard (66), we came to Glendora, several miles west of Claremont. This city was named in 1887 by combining the word "glen" and the last four letters of the feminine name, Leadora. It was in that year that the railroad reached the newly-named town. Also in 1887, the first lot was sold in Glendora, an event commemorated by a stone marker at the corner of Glendora Avenue and Bennett Avenue.

In 1911 Glendora was incorporated as a city. During the following years the economy of Glendora was based on the production of citrus. The city grew slowly, and in 1950 the population was 4,000. Beginning in the late 1950s, Glendora experienced rapid growth, and by 1990 the population of this residential city had increased to 47,832.

Glendora is the home of what is believed to be the largest bougainvillea in the United States. This tremendous ornamental vine, with its purple-red floral bracts, was planted in 1901, and for nearly a century since then has continued to grow. On January 7, 1978, the Glendora Bougainvillea became a State of California Historical Landmark. A month after this, on February 7, 1978, this bougainvillea was entered on the National Register of Historic Places.

After our visit to Glendora, we continued to Azusa, situated near the entrance to San Gabriel Canyon. This area was deeded by the Mexican Government to Louis Arenas in 1841. In 1844 Rancho Azusa was sold to Henry Dalton, who had recently arrived from England. Under Dalton's ownership, the rancho developed and began to grow after Dalton installed an irrigation system, planted vineyards, and built a flour mill.

In 1854, gold was discovered in San Gabriel Canyon, and for the next two decades mining activity continued until the gold was depleted. The first lots were sold in Azusa in 1886, and the first plan for the town was drawn up in 1887. Business places were soon started, including a grocery store and a newspaper. In 1891 a bank opened its doors in the small town, and a high school was established in that year. On December 29, 1898, Azusa was incorporated as a city, and the first mayor took office.

By the early years of the twentieth century, citrus became an important industry in Azusa. Population growth was slow until the 1950s, then increased during the years that followed. In 1990 the census showed that the population of Azusa was 41,203.

Duarte, "City of Health — Home of the City of Hope," as announced by a sign at the entrance to the city, was our next destination as we traveled to the west. On May 10, 1841, while still under the control of the Mexican Government, Andres Duarte received a grant of land, part of which later became the town of Duarte.

Largely an agricultural town during the first years after it was settled, Duarte grew slowly during the late 1800s and early 1900s. It became the home of the City of Hope, founded in 1913. This medical facility had its start in two tents that were set up on a few acres of desert in Duarte, northeast of Los Angeles.

The City of Hope is designated as a Clinical Cancer Research Center by the National Cancer Institute. It is dedicated to the prevention, treatment, and cure of cancer and other diseases that are life-threatening.

The population of Duarte had reached 6,000 by 1957, and on August 22 of that year the city of Duarte was incorporated.

During the 1920s a federal program of numbered national highways was started, and on November 11, 1926, Route 66 became part of this system. Chicago, Illinois was the starting point in the east, and the highway went through eight states to Los Angeles: Illinois, Missouri, Kansas, Oklahoma, Texas, New Mexico, Arizona, and California.

On September 21, 1996, the city of Duarte celebrated the 70th anniversary of Route 66 with a "Salute to Route 66" Parade. There were more than 100 entries, and among these were marching bands, antique and classic cars, motorcycles, floats, equestrian units, various civic organizations, and churches.

Among the California cities that we visited on our trip, we noted the following in the published parade lineup: Arcadia, Azusa, Monrovia, Rancho Cucamonga, and Victorville, in addition to Duarte. Each of these cities had at least one entry in this commemorative parade.

We continued to the west on Route 66 from Duarte to the adjoining city of Monrovia. Historic Route 66 follows Huntington Drive through these cities.

In 1886, William N. Monroe, a construction engineer for the railroad, laid out the town site of Monrovia, with the help of his associates. Soon after this the town was named for him. The following year, on December 8, 1887, Monrovia was incorporated. The city is located below the San Gabriel Mountains. Monrovia Peak, more than a mile above sea level, lies northeast of the city.

For several decades after Monrovia was founded, much of the area was agricultural, and citrus was a principal crop. Like other cities on the route we have followed, Monrovia participated in the population growth of California during the years after the Second World War. The census count in 1990 was 35,733.

After Monrovia, the next city that we visited was Arcadia, immediately to the west. In 1875, Elias Jackson Baldwin purchased 8,000 acres of Rancho Santa Anita, and Arcadia was founded here in 1888. The town was laid out by Herman A. Unruh, a railroad official, and named for Arcadia, a rural area of ancient Greece.

The town was incorporated August 5, 1903, when the population was 360, and E. J. Baldwin became the first Mayor. After the First World War, the population of Arcadia increased rapidly during the decade of the 1920s. Growth slowed during the 1930s, but after World War II, as the population of California grew at a rapid pace, Arcadia shared in this growth. The census showed a population of 48,284 in 1990.

The Los Angeles State and County Arboretum is located in Arcadia on the west side of Baldwin Avenue, just south of Foothill Freeway. There are many acres of trees and shrubs, a bird sanctuary, greenhouses, and several historic buildings here. East of Baldwin Avenue, across from the Arboretum, is the well-known thoroughbred horse racing track, Santa Anita Park, situated on West Huntington Drive.

We left Arcadia, and entered Pasadena, home of the Tournament of Roses Parade and the Rose Bowl Game, held each year on New Year's Day.

Pasadena was first settled in 1873 by a group of Indiana colonists, and Pasadena became the name of the community on April 22, 1875. In the two years since the first settlers had arrived, Pasadena grew rapidly, and had become a city. Several years later, on June 19, 1886, Pasadena was incorporated. January 1, 1890, was the date of Pasadena's first "Festival of Roses" parade, comprised largely of decorated carriages. After the turn of the century, Pasadena continued to grow, and by 1910, the city had more than 30,000 inhabitants.

Following the first Parade held on New Year's Day, 1890, the number of Parade entrants increased each year. In 1895, the Pasadena Tournament of Roses Association was established to manage the annual Parade. A century later, in the mid-1990s, this volunteer non-profit organization had about 935 members.

The first Rose Bowl Game was played in 1902, in Tournament Park, between the University of Michigan and Stanford University. Michigan won the game, 49-0.

The city of Pasadena has preserved many of its historic buildings that are located in the original business district, Old Pasadena. Listed as a Historic District in the National Register of Historic Places, this eleven-block area contains many buildings that were built in the last years of the nineteenth century, or soon after 1900. Altogether there are more than 400 buildings in Pasadena that are listed in the National Register of Historic Places.

The population of Pasadena continued to grow in the decades after World War II, and in 1990 the census was 131,586.

After enjoying our overnight visit to Pasadena, our route was to the southwest, and soon we were in South Pasadena. Mapped out in 1885, the town was incorporated March 2, 1888. Situated four miles northeast of Los Angeles, the area of the city of South Pasadena is between three and four square miles. In 1990, the census showed a population of 23,936.

We continued toward the southwest after leaving South Pasadena, and the highway took us into Los Angeles, and to the Santa Monica Freeway. Following this westward, we reached Culver City after a few miles.

In 1914, Harry H. Culver arrived in this area from Nebraska, and, after acquiring land, started the town that is now Culver City, named in his honor. Originally a residential community, a number of industries developed, and the population increased. The census of 1990 showed 38,793 inhabitants.

On this morning, near the end of our trip, we left Culver City and soon entered Santa Monica, the westernmost city of our cross-country trip. We drove to the beach, and while we were there I took a photograph with the Pacific Ocean on the horizon, as I had with the Atlantic Ocean in the east.

A few settlers were in the Santa Monica area at an earlier date, but it was in July, 1875, that the first lots were sold, and the town developed after that date. In less than a year, the population of

Santa Monica had grown to a thousand people, and many houses had been built.

Population growth was not continuous after the first year, and by 1880 there was a decline in population to less than 450 inhabitants. After this there was an increase in population, and in late 1886 the voters decided in favor of incorporation. During the next year the state legislature established Santa Monica as an incorporated city.

The building of aircraft became an important industry in Santa Monica beginning early in the 1920s. Thousands of passenger and military airplanes were built here during the following decades. The city grew rapidly in the World War II years, and this growth continued. In 1990 the population of Santa Monica was 86,905.

After our visit to Santa Monica, we started toward our home in Arizona and stayed that night in Costa Mesa. It was a good feeling for both of us to know that we had completed our trip from ocean to ocean.

The next day we continued southward and stopped briefly at Mission San Juan Capistrano. At San Diego we took the Interstate Highway to the east, through El Cajon and El Centro, to Yuma, Arizona, where we stayed overnight. We arrived at our home in Tucson, early in the afternoon of the following day, and we were glad to be home safely after a long trip.

Postscript

This trip across the United States in 1992 worked out as we anticipated when we made our plans. We were able to see parts of the United States that would have been missed if we had traveled only on high speed Interstate Highways.

It was our plan after this cross-country trip that we would publish a book about it. During the next two years, I finished nearly all of the library research, and the manuscript was partially completed.

We lived in Arizona seventeen years after moving there, then returned to Ohio and moved to Gahanna, a suburb of Columbus. The move back to Ohio was for family reasons, as our daughter, Sandra, was retiring after 33 years as a Federal employee. We also had other family ties that made it better to return.

Although she was active and lived a normal life, Gertrude had a health problem during our last few years in Arizona. In 1990, malignant lymph nodes were found and, because of this, the oncologist prescribed daily medication.

After our move to Gahanna late in 1994, she was under the care of an oncologist in Columbus. He had her Arizona health records, of course, and after laboratory tests, he prescribed a series of chemotherapy treatments. For a few months her condition seemed to be improving, but after more than a year of chemotherapy, her health failed and lymphoma became fatal, on April 15, 1996.

Many months went by after April, 1996, before I could believe that I would be able to finish this book. Finally, I realized that the book should be written. I slowly completed the manuscript, then arranged with the publisher to have the book printed.

Index

Arnold, MD, 15
Arrow Rock, MO, 97, 98, 100, 102
Arthur, Chester A.,
    President, 31
Ash Fork, AZ, 163, 164
Atlanta, GA, 115, 116
Atlantic Coast, 13
Atlantic Coastal Plain, 11
Atlantic Ocean, 9, 11, 12, 13, 52,
    172, 184
Atwater, 48
Augusta County, VA, 99
Augusta, ME, 31
Aull, John, James
    and Robert, 103
Azusa, CA, 181, 182
Bakersfield, CA, 173
Baldwin, Christopher C., 46
Baldwin, Elias Jackson, 183
Baldwin, John, 111
Baldwin City, KS, 111
Baltimore and
    Ohio Railroad, 23
Baltimore, MD, 11, 14, 15, 16, 17,
    21
Barstow, CA, 172, 173, 174
Barstow College, 173
Barton, Clara, 118
Barton, Stephen, 118
Barton County, KS, 118, 119
Beallsville, PA, 31, 32
Beard, Charles Austin, 64
Beardstown, IL, 82
Beatty, Zacheus, 45
Becknell, William, 97, 98, 112, 119,
    135
Bedous, France, 89
Beeson, Henry, 28
Belen, NM, 143, 144

Bellemont, AZ, 160
Belleville, IL, 88
Belleville, IN, 74
Belmont County, OH, 42, 43, 45
Benevola, MD, 21
Bent, Charles, 130, 131
Bent, William, 130, 131
Bent County, CO, 129
Bent, St. Vrain
    & Company, 130
Bent's Old Fort National
    Historic Site, 129, 130, 135
Bernalillo, NM, 141
Bernalillo County, NM, 142, 147
Bernardo, NM, 144
Bethany College, 116
Bethesda, MD, 18, 19, 20
Bible (Bethesda)-
    (Jerusalem), 19
Bible (Rehoboth), 11
Bicycles, 55, 56
Big Timbers, 128
Bill Williams, 160
Bill Williams Mountain, 160
Bingham, Geoge Caleb, 99
Birds, Flight of, 56
Birthplace of the Tomato, 51
Bishop, Dr. Robert H., 33
Bison, 48
Black Hawk War, 83. 94
Black Mountains, 165
Blaine, Ephraim Lyon, 29, 30
Blaine, James Gillespie, 30, 31
Bluewater, NM, 150
Bluff City, IL, 81, 85
Bond, Shadrach, 78, 86
Bond County, IL, 86
Boone, Daniel, 96
Boone County, MO, 96
Boonsboro, MD, 20, 21

190

Carlton, KS, 115
Caroline County, MD, 13
Caroline County, VA, 91
Carson, Christopher (Kit), 99, 129,
   130, 132
Carter, Jimmy
   (James Earl), President, 156
Casa Blanca, NM, 147
Casa de Rancho
   Cucamonga, 178
Casey, Robert P., 25
Casey, Zadok, 79
Casey, IL, 79
Casselman River, 23
Cathedral of St.
   Francis of Assisi, 140
Catoctin Mountain, 20
Caton, Richard, 16
Catonsville, MD, 16
Catron, Thomas Benton, 146
Catron County, NM, 145
Celeron, 36
Centerville, IN, 62, 63
Central Plains, 49
Central Public Library,
   St. Louis, MO, 47
Chaco Culture
   National Historical Park, 151
Chalk Hill, PA, 27
Chambers, AZ, 157, 158
Chambless, CA, 170, 171
Champaign County, OH, 53
Chapel of Our Lady of
   Light, (Loretto Chapel), 141
Charleston, KS, 122
Charleston, SC, 39
Charleston, WV, 40
Charlottesville, IN, 64
Charlottesville, VA, 34, 53, 90
Chase, KS, 117

Chautauquas, 46
Chesapeake Bay, 11, 13, 14,1 5, 23
Chesapeake Bay Bridge, 11, 14
Chester, IL, 88
Chestnut Ridge, 27
Cheyenne tribe, 107, 128
Chicago, IL, 46, 77, 79, 115, 163,
   171, 174, 176, 182
Chihuahua, Mexico, 98
Chillicothe, OH, 42, 43, 47, 50
China, 28, 111
Chinese, 111
Choptank River, 13
Chouteau, Auguste, 89
Chouteau's Island, 124
Churchill, Winston, 96
Cibola County, NM, 147, 150
Cibola National Forest, 142, 146
Cimarron Branch, Santa
   Fe Trail, 134
Cimarron Cut-off, 122, 135
Cimarron Desert, 98
Cimarron, KS, 122
Cincinnati College, 33
Cincinnati, OH, 33, 44, 53, 80
City of Hope, 181
Civilian Conservation
   Corps, 20
Civil War, 17, 21, 39, 44, 64, 71,
   95, 99, 102, 111, 117, 118, 120,
   122, 123, 136, 139, 141
Claremont, Ca, 180
Claremont Colleges, 180
Clark, George Rogers, 53, 59, 60,
   61, 75, 78, 79, 91
Clark, William, 91, 92, 93
Clark Center, IL, 79
Clark County, IL, 79
Clark County, IN, 67
Clark County, OH, 53

193

Cucamonga Peak, 177
Cucamonga Rancho, 178
Culver, Harry H., 184
Culver City, CA, 184
Cumberland, IN, 67
Cumberland, MD, 21, 22, 31, 37, 38, 39, 49, 86
Cumberland County, IL, 79
Cumberland Road, 22, 38, 43, 67, 79, 85, 86
Daggett, John, 172
Daggett, CA, 172
Dalton, Henry, 181
Danby, CA, 170
Danville, IN, 74
Danville, MO, 95
Danville, Va, 95
Datil, NM, 146
Daughters of the American Revolution, 32, 100
Dawes Arboretum, 49
Dayton, Jonathan, 55
Dayton, OH, 55, 56, 57, 58
Dearborn County, IN, 67
Decatur, IL, 82
Declaration of Independence, 26, 64
Deerfield, KS, 124
Delavan, IL, 114
Delavan, KS, 114
Delaware, 9, 10, 11, 12
Delaware Bay, 9
Delaware Coast, 11, 16
Delaware Indians, 31, 45, 107
Delaware, OH, 50
Delaware River, 35
Delaware tribe, 74, 108
Demint, James, 53
Democratic, 104

Denton, MD, 13
Denver, James William, 126
Denver, CO, 126, 127
Detroit, MI, 60
Devore, CA, 175
Dexter, IL, 80
Dexter Methodist Church, 80
Dickinson, Daniel S., 114
Dickinson County, KS, 114
District of Columbia, 17, 19
Dixon, Jeremiah, 35
Dodge, Henry I., 121
Dodge City, KS, 98, 119, 121, 122, 137
Doniphan, Waddel, 103
Douglas, Stephan A., 110
Douglas County, KS, 110
Dover, DE, 9, 11
Dover, MO, 101
Drake, Francis, 167
Drake's Bay, 167
Duarte, Andres, 181
Duarte, CA, 181, 182
Dublin, IN, 63
Dunreith, IN, 64
East Coast, 108
East Germantown, IN, 63
East St. Louis, IL, 88
Eaton, William, 58
Eaton, OH, 58
Eckhart Mines, MD, 22
Eden, Sir Robert, 13
Edgerton, KS, 110
Edwards, Ninian, 78
Edwards, William C., 120
Edwards County, KS, 120
Edwardsville, IL, 87
Effingham, Earl of, 80
Effingham, IL, 80
Effingham County, IL, 80

201

McGuffey School District, 34
McGuffey, William Holmes, 33, 34
McHenry, James, 15
McIntire, John, 47
McKinley, William,
    President, 29, 151
McKinley County, NM, 151
McNair, Alexander, 93
McPherson, James Birdseye, 115,
    116
McPherson, KS, 116, 117, 122
McPherson County, KS, 115, 116,
    117
McQuilkin, Samuel, 75
Medal of Freedom, 95
Meigs County, OH, 44
Memorial Bridge, William
    Preston Lane, Jr., 14
Memphis, TN, 82, 172
Menard, Pierre, 78
Mesita, NM, 147
Meteor Crater, 158, 159
Mexican, 98, 135, 137, 140, 141,
    144, 154, 168, 178, 179, 181
Mexico, 98, 117, 130, 135, 138,
    140, 141, 146, 154, 168
Mexico City, Mexico, 168
Miami County, OH, 54
Miami tribe, 74
Miami Univsersity, 33, 34
Micheltorena, Manuel, 168
Middletown, MD, 20
Middle Wheeling Creek, 38
Midway, MO, 96
Milan, NM, 150
Miller, A.B., 177
Millersburg, MO, 96
Mineola, MO, 95
Minter, William, 52

Mission Basilica San
    Diego de Alcala, 167
Mission of San Miguel of
    Santa Fe, 140
Mission San Gabriel
    Arcangel, 167
Mission San Juan
    Capistrano, 167, 185
Mississippi River, 43, 48, 59, 69,
    77, 78, 82, 87, 88, 89, 90, 92,
    94, 96, 108, 113, 118, 137, 172
Mississippi Valley, 52
Missouri, 49, 89, 92, 93, 94, 95, 96,
    97, 98, 99, 100, 101, 102, 103,
    108, 109, 111, 125, 135, 168,
    182
Missourians, 99
Missouri River, 91, 93, 94, 96, 97,
    98, 100, 101, 102, 105, 106,
    118
Mitchell, George, 12
Mitchell Caverns Natural
    Preserve, 170
Model, CO, 131
Mohave County, AZ, 153, 164
Mojave, CA, 172, 173
Mojave Desert, 170, 172, 174
Mojave Indians, 169
Mojave River, 174
Monk's Mound, 88
Monocacy, Battle of, 18
Monocacy River, 16
Monongahela, Battle of the, 26
Monogahela River, 29, 31, 35
Monroe, James, President, 27, 93
Monroe, William N., 182
Monrovia, CA, 182, 183
Monrovia Peak, 182
Montana, 172
Monterey, CA, 167, 168

Monterey Bay, 167
Montgomery, Richard, 55, 95
Montgomery City, MO, 95
Montgomery County
    Historical Society, 57
Montgomery County, KS, 109
Montgomery County, MD, 18
Montgomery County, MO, 95
Montgomery County, OH, 55, 95
Montrose, IL, 80
Monument Place Bridge, 39
Mora, NM, 134
Mora County, NM, 134, 137
Mora River, 134
Morgan, John H., 44, 45, 72
Mormon Battalion, 116, 154
Mormons, 174, 175, 176
Morris, Thomas, 112
Morris County, KS, 112
Morristown, OH, 43
Mountain Branch, Santa Fe
    Trail, 134, 135, 136
Mountain State, 40
Mountain Time Zone, 124
Mount Auburn, IN, 63
Mount Elbert, 125
Mount Katahdin, 20
Mount Meridian, IN, 74
Mount Olivet Cemetery, 17
Mount Sunflower, 109
Mount Taylor, 147
Mount Union College, 29
Mount Vernon, VA, 14
Mount Washington Tavern, 27
Mount Whitney, 125
Mulberry Grove, IL, 86
Museum of Northern Arizona, 160
Muskingum College, 46
Muskingum County, OH, 43, 45,
    47, 49

Muskingum River, 41, 47, 48
Nanticoke River, 12
Natchez, MS, 82
National Anthem, 16
National City, CA, 174
National Highway, 40
National Old Trails
    Road, The, 31, 129, 171
National Park Service, 27, 139
National Park System, 120, 136
National Pike, 22, 38
National Radio Astronomy
    Observatory-Very
    Large Array, 145
National Register of
    Historic Places, 137, 181, 184
National Road, 22, 25, 27, 33, 37,
    38, 39, 43, 45, 47, 48, 49, 51,
    54, 55, 63, 67, 70, 74, 79, 86
National Road/Zane Grey
    Museum, 46
Nation's Highway, A, 63
Navajo, AZ, 158
Navajo County, AZ, 156, 157, 158
Navajo Indian Reservation, 151,
    158
Nebraska, 107, 184
Needles, CA, 169, 170, 171, 173
Nemacolin, 31, 32
Nemacolin's Path, 31, 39
Nemacolin's Trail, 31
Neosho River, 112
Nevada, 107, 172, 173
New Albion, 167
Newark, OH, 49, 50
Newberry Springs, CA, 172
New Castle, IN, 64
New Castle County, DE, 11
New Concord, OH, 45, 46
New England, 122, 134

New Florence, MO, 95
New Franklin, MO, 97, 100
New Haven, CT, 64
New Hope, OH, 58
New Lebanon, OH, 58
New Madrid, MO, 92
New Market, MD, 16
New Mexico, 98, 130, 131, 133, 134, 135, 136, 139, 140, 141, 142, 143, 144, 146, 147, 149, 150, 151, 153, 154, 155, 157, 158, 168, 173, 182
New Mexico Institute of Mining and Technology, 144
New Orleans, LA, 78, 82, 89
New Orleans, LA, Battle of, 103
New Salem, (Menard County), IL, 82, 84
New Westville, OH, 58
New York, NY, 66, 134
New York, State of, 114, 122
Niebuhr, Reinhold, 94
Nobel Peace Prize, 29
North, 17
North America, 26, 41, 139
North American Birds, 149
North Carolina, 56, 67, 87, 95, 172
North Dakota, 91
Northern Arizona University, 160
Northern Panhandle, 35
Northwest, 104
Northwest Territory, 42, 48, 53, 54, 79
Norwich, OH, 46
Oak Creek Canyon, 162
Oatman, AZ, 165
Offerle, Laurence, 120
Offerle, KS, 120
Ogden, IN, 64

Ohio, 9, 17, 22, 25, 33, 35, 40, 41, 42, 43, 44, 45, 46, 47, 48, 49, 50, 51, 52, 54, 57, 58, 62, 70, 72, 79, 86, 92, 111, 112, 138, 161
Ohio and Erie Canal, 49
Ohioans, 44
Ohio Buckeye tree, 52
Ohio County, WV, 36, 39
Ohio Historical Marker, 54
Ohio Historical Society, 46
Ohio River, 22, 35, 36, 38, 39, 40, 41, 42, 43, 44, 49, 53, 59, 62, 63, 67, 69, 70, 72, 77, 79, 93
Ohio River Valley, 39
Ohio State University, 52
O'Keeffe, Georgia, 142
Okalahoma, 108, 119, 123, 131, 136, 173, 182
Oklahoma Panhandle, 137
Olathe, KS, 110
Olathe Town Company, 110
Old Couch Inn, 49
Old Courthouse Museum, 57
Old National Trail Highway, 170, 171
Old Town, Albuquerque, 142
Old Trails Monument, 169
Old Washington, OH, 44, 45
Olentangy River, 50
Omaha, NE, 91
Omega, NM, 146
Ordinance of 1787, 41, 43
Oregon, 91, 104, 107
Oregon Trail, 104, 106, 107, 110
Osage City, KS, 111
Osage County, KS, 111
Osage Indians, 112, 114
Osage tribe, 107, 112

211